Country Ways

in Hampshire & Dorset

Country Ways

in Hampshire & Dorset

ANTHONY HOWARD

Countryside Books/TVS

First Published 1986
© Text Anthony Howard 1986

All rights reserved.
No reproduction permitted
without the prior consent
of the publishers:

Countryside Books
3 Catherine Road,
Newbury, Berkshire.

ISBN 0 905392 66 3

Front Cover Photograph: OSF Picture Library
Back Cover Photograph: Derek Budd

Photographs by Derek Budd and Tony Nutley, with additional pictures
by Harry Ashley (pages 45, 77) and Robin Fletcher (page 10)

Produced through MRM (Print Consultants) Ltd., Reading
Typeset by Acorn Bookwork, Salisbury
Printed in England by Borcombe Printers, Romsey

CONTENTS

INTRODUCTION

There is still much that is beautiful, much that is unspoilt, much that is quiet and much that is private in the countryside of Southern England. *Country Ways* takes some of the loveliest parts of the South of England and examines them through the eyes of country folk with their roots deep in their local area. The sense of history is strong in these places, and there is still a sureness and quiet confidence about the places and the people, built on the foundations of old tradition and ancient families. It is a feeling which may well have disappeared within a couple of generations, and which should be recorded before the people themselves have joined their forefathers in the village cemeteries. It is a sense of the past, which their grandchildren may not begin to understand. It is a sense of tradition, without which the future will be the poorer.

The neighbouring counties of Hampshire and Dorset offer as wide a variety of soils, wildlife and natural history as it is possible to find in the South of England. Writing of Dorset in 1858 John Pouncy thought that there was 'every probability that a considerable time will elapse before the tone and general characteristics of the county undergo any material change'. And, even today, from Shaftesbury through Sturminster Newton and down to Bridport and from Lyme Regis across to Wimborne, there is still a sense of remoteness and solitude. Hampshire, on the other hand, with the industry of Southampton, Basingstoke and Portsmouth, together with the wealth of Winchester and the sophistication of its Northern uplands is a far busier and more bustling scene. But in both counties, if you will just take the trouble to turn off the main roads and head for villages, of which you have never heard and which sometimes may not even appear on your road map, you will still find unspoilt scenery to charm your eye and, in the pubs, churches and on the farms, you will meet quiet and dignified people, whose families go back for many generations and who hold firm to their links with the past. It is these people who tell their simple stories in *Country Ways*.

The spectacular Purbeck scenery is dominated by Corfe Castle.

A Stonechat, photographed in the New Forest. This heathland bird with its characteristic black head and rust coloured chest has its nest on the ground among dried bracken and heather.

There have always been deer in the New Forest, the Royal Forest of the Chase. The bucks are seen at their best in September when the velvet protecting the antlers drops off in readiness for the rut.

THE NEW FOREST

IF you look North and West across the Avon Valley from Woodgreen on the Northern edge of Hampshire's New Forest, you can see lush pastures stretching away into the distance towards Salisbury and Shaftesbury. Even in the pale sunshine of a winter's morning the water meadows look prosperous and colourful. By contrast, if you look South and East, you are faced by the sombre prospect of the New Forest with its gaunt heathlands and hungry soils.

In spite of its name, the New Forest is over nine hundred years old. And, with Nature overcoming the poor quality of the land, it is still a haven for wild life, trees, plants and flowers. Writing in 1598, John Manwood described it as 'a territorie of wooddy and fruitful pastures, privileged for wild beasts and foules of Forest, Chase and Warren, to rest and abide in the safe protection of the King for his Princely delight'.

Queen Victoria decided to give the Forest back to the people of her country. At the same time, she also let loose some Arab stallions, which she had been given. These splendid but refined creatures diluted the blood of the hardy New Forest ponies, which had been able to survive quite cheerfully on gorse, bracken and brambles. Today the ponies need grass. When the grass is not growing on the sandy soil, there are many sad and stringy horses.

Despite the occasional shortage of food, one of the great joys of the New Forest is the animals – cattle, pigs, donkeys and geese, as well as ponies – which can wander freely over its acres. If you are driving through the area at night you may be annoyed when the car coming the opposite way does not dip its lights. Perhaps it will be some consolation to know that the driver is almost certainly a forester. A black cow on a macadam road on a dark night is nearly invisible, and it is in those split seconds when two cars are passing that the damage is often done. Scores of animals are killed and maimed each year.

The people of the Forest – the real foresters – are as different from the people who live in the rest of Hampshire as the people of Romney Marsh are from those who live in the rest of Kent. Forest customs are legion. Traditions go back through generations. It is sometimes said that it is more important to have been born on the right side of the cattle grid than on the right side of the blanket. There are some Forest gypsies, who claim with confidence that King Rufus was not killed at the well-marked Rufus Stone, but a couple of miles away at Stoney Cross. They justify their belief by saying that the information has been handed down through their family for over 900 years. It is this sense of timelessness, which gives so much fascination to the ancient parts of Southern England. With a little imagination, it is possible to roll back the centuries and to experience life as it was a thousand years ago.

The small farmers, who live in the Forest, are called commoners. Economic necessity demands that most of them have jobs in addition to their farming. Theirs are the animals which wander wild across the heathland and along the roads. In the autumn, if you are very lucky, you may see thirty or forty of them on horseback, rounding up scores of ponies at a time for branding and marking. It is a scene straight out of the Wild West.

ONE of the best known of the commoners is Hugh Pasmore from Fritham. He and his wife, Margaret, seem to relish their lot, even in the foulest weather. Striding along in the rain with the cowl of his sopping duffle-coat covering his head and with his tall, slim figure leaning into the prevailing wind, he looks like nothing so much as a medieval monk. 'On a wild, February day, you think you're mad to be slogging around in the mud and the filth. It is even worse when it snows and you get snowed up. But I don't know – once you start doing it, you just can't give it up. We started some thirty-five years ago. We bought a couple of mares and we got so keen on it that we finished up by having eighty mares on the Forest. Well, we've cut 'em down now. We've got a dozen. But it sometimes does make you wonder why you want to do it. It's just a way of life, I think. Once you've done it, you can't bear to be without some form of animals around you.'

Commoners pay a marking fee of ten pounds a year for each animal they keep loose on the forest land. 'Anybody who has a place in the New Forest, to which Common Rights are attached, can turn out any number of animals. It doesn't matter if you've only got half an acre – you can turn out a hundred animals. In fact, there are just three thousand altogether on the Forest now. That's sixteen hundred head of cattle and the rest of them are ponies. That's about seven hundred and fifty less than there were three years ago. Economics come into that. People can't make money out of ponies on the Forest now as they could in the old days, so that, inevitably, they're not going to keep so many.'

Hugh Pasmore is quick to underline the vital role which his wife plays. 'I don't think honestly that you could do this single-handed. She works just as hard as I do – sometimes a jolly sight harder. You see, you've got all sorts of things. Mucking out the stables; carting the hay. We make about fifteen acres of hay. She carts bales around just the same as I do. You just wouldn't want to keep as many horses as we do if you didn't have a helper. And you certainly couldn't afford to have a paid helper, so your wife comes in very handy in that way.'

Commoners' animals face many dangers – and not just on the New Forest Roads. There is also the threat of theft and rustling, and the possibility of natural accidents

Hugh Pasmore, a commoner in the New Forest for thirty-five years, sawing logs at his home near Fritham.

to animals as they wander far from their homes. All these hazards create big problems for people trying to make a living out of cattle and ponies, when they're running unfenced on the Forest. But not all commoners take the same risks as Hugh Pasmore. 'I was fool enough one night to get up and see some poachers' lights out in the fields. So I went down to tackle them. I got as far as the second field. There was the buck in the hedge with the dogs attacking it. I drove them off, and then these fellows with their searchlights shone them in my eyes. Another fellow tackled me from behind. He knocked four teeth out, split my face open and really gave me a rough time of it. But, since then, I don't think they've been back very often. And next time, we shall phone the police first before going out. I learnt my lesson then.'

One of the great joys for the Pasmores is being able to ride straight out onto the Forest from their home. 'Your animals take you into the Forest. Even on a really dirty day, when normally you would probably sit in front of a fire, if you've got animals you've got to do something about them. So you go out. And that is the great point about it. You see more of the Forest and you see it in all its moods. In the winter it

Margaret Pasmore feeding one of her ponies. One of the great joys for the Pasmores is being able to ride straight out onto the Forest from their home.

can be awful. In the summer and in May or June it's marvellous. And, if you're interested in flowers and birds, you've got the hedgerows and the trees. I think it's your animals that give you an opportunity to take part in the way of life in the Forest.'

THERE have always been deer in the New Forest. For most of its history its role has been as a Royal Forest of the Chase. Those who killed the deer were themselves executed without compunction. Today, Forest keeper Derek Thompson culls the deer as part of his job. But he also has the skill of being able to summon them with his foghorn voice, aided sometimes by a bit of bribery in the form of potatoes and other food. Derek is a short, cheerful man with a handsome grey/green uniform, and ageless eyes that have spent hundreds of hours watching out for his precious charges.

On a lucky day, and provided that you keep very still, you can watch as scores of nimble and delicate fallow deer surround the keeper and accept his offerings. 'They'll eat the maize to start with. That's the first choice, and then go on to the cattle cake or potatoes a bit later. Their winter coat is that sort of dirty, what we call mulberry, colour. In summertime, of course, they've got that lovely, reddish-coloured spotted coat. Early September is the time to see them really, when the bucks are in their best antlers and their best coats. They look so good then. They drop their antlers about March or April time, and then, within two or three days, the new ones start growing. They start off as little buttons and gradually get bigger until the end of August or September when the velvet, which is protecting the antlers, drops off and they've got their new set of antlers for the rut.'

Sometimes, as he feeds the deer, they will be briefly upset as a pair of frisky New Forest ponies canter by. But then, you might glance away for a couple of seconds and, when you look back, the whole herd will have vanished into the thicket as though Derek Thompson has performed some gigantic conjuring trick.

ON the western side of the Forest near Linwood is a tiny woodman's cottage at the bottom of a gravel track. It is a remote and delightful spot and the home of naturalist and wildlife photographer Robin Fletcher. He is a chunky figure, usually clad in khaki, and always with camera and binoculars slung round his neck. 'I'm surrounded by deer and wildlife of every kind, equally in the harsh winter months and in the heat of the summer. In winter, feeding the birds is a particular delight. I watch them squabbling over the peanuts when I come down to make my morning tea. An hour later I find I've forgotten all about the tea and I haven't even lit the gas. Tits are commonest – blue tits, great tits, coal tits and marsh tits. Usually there are nuthatches, chaffinches and greenfinches, and, of course, blackbirds, robins and hedge sparrows. Sometimes siskins or a woodpecker. Occasionally, they all vanish miraculously. In a deathly hush a sparrowhawk knifes his way through for a quick grab. Squirrels come by and help themselves too. And they're all real friends and neighbours to me.

'Just down the track from my back door there's an old tree stump, which conceals evidence of some other hungry neighbours. Piles of cherry stones, hidden there by a wood mouse, and gnawed open in private for the juicy kernels.'

Robin is up at all hours in every season to snatch his wildlife photographs. Often he has to wait patiently and for long spells in the cold and the damp. Sometimes his patience is in vain, and he goes away empty-handed. But now and again his skill and stoicism bring their reward. 'Not far from where I live, there's an ordinary-looking forest pond. It dries up in the summer and curiously, for that reason, it shelters some rare creatures. One of them is called an Apus and is a very primitive form of crustacean distantly related to lobsters, crabs and shrimps. The pond may well be the only place in Britain where it exists. There are also fairy shrimps. Although they are not as rare as the Apus, they are far from an everyday spectacle. If these fascinating creatures lived in a pond that did not dry up in the hot weather they would probably be unable to compete with the ordinary pond life in permanent water. Apparently their survival depends on the summer dry-out. At that time, all the adults of both species perish, but their eggs in vast numbers can withstand prolonged drought, where they lie in the bottom of the pond. When the ponds dry out completely some eggs blow away for miles. Others travel vast distances in mud on a bird's foot – perhaps then hatching months or years later in a cart-rut or a puddle in an old tree stump.'

On Robin's frequent walks through the Forest on the winding gravel tracks that lead away from his cottage, he can point out a thousand things that might escape the notice of a casual visitor. 'When you see bent and crippled trees in the Forest, it is often the work of squirrels. They gnaw off the young bark in the Spring to get at the sap. Even though the trees usually survive, they're useless in any real sense after such an assault. And, in the harsh way that Nature often operates, it is not just animal predators which attack trees. If you look carefully when you are out walking you will notice some trees which have grown like corkscrews. Believe it or not, this damage is caused by sweet-smelling honeysuckle with its amazingly strong vine. As the tree grows and expands, the vine cuts into the wood and leaves it permanently twisted.

'The exotic, hour-glass figures of some of the bushes in the open forest are not some sexy prank of Nature. They are normal shrubs which have been nibbled at year after year by deer and ponies. Each year the new shoots are bitten hard back, promoting slow, dense growth. Eventually, the top-most shoots grow beyond reach and develop normally. But the wasp waist-line persists at around nibbling level.'

Even on the ground, fed by centuries of dead leaves, there are clues to the nature of plants and animals. 'The woodland floors in winter are mostly just carpeted with brown leaves, brightened occasionally by a patch of moss. Everything faintly green and juicy has disappeared into the relentless jaws of the ponies, cattle and deer – except for two sorts of plants, which look quite appetising. Their soft, green leaves showing no signs of nibbling, the foxglove and the wood-spurge are well set to get away to a good start in the spring. The reason is that they are both poisonous and taste awful.'

Nearby is a bush so spiky that it makes the gorse, which grows everywhere in the Forest, seem quite tame by comparison. 'Butcher's broom is an evergreen plant quite common in the area. The ponies sometimes eat holly, and even gorse, but they seldom touch butcher's broom because it is so dry and stringy. Butchers used to make it into a short besom for cleaning their chopping-blocks. The spines on the plant are so keen that no fragment of meat escaped.'

IT is always most pleasant to visit the New Forest and to enjoy its wild and lonely expanses in the spring, summer and autumn. The advantage of being there in the winter is that the roads are clear and the tourists are at home. Certainly, in the bad months, it can be cold and wet and miserable. But it can also be bright and shining and crystal clear. And there are always plenty of fascinating things happening, both in the world of Nature and in the world of man. You only have to take the trouble to slow down and look for them.

New Forest cattle grazing. Commoners pay a marking fee of ten pounds a year for each animal they keep loose on the Forest land.

THE ISLE OF WIGHT

THE ferry journey from Lymington to Yarmouth on the Isle of Wight holds all the exhilaration of a trip to a foreign country. It may only be a short distance, but there is something pleasantly alien about the place and its people. It is no wonder that it is seen by tens of thousands of holiday-makers as a perfect opportunity to travel 'abroad' to a country where the people happen to speak the English language.

Whether those stalwart and dedicated islanders, who love the gentle hills, the sea views and the winding lanes enough to get up at dawn each working day to commute to the mainland to do their work, feel that they are leaving and returning to foreign shores is hard to judge. But people as different as Jane Austen and Karl Marx have sung the Isle of Wight's praises. Marx described it as 'a little paradise' in 1874, and in *Mansfield Park* Jane Austen wrote, 'She thinks of nothing but the Isle of Wight, and she calls it The Island, as if there were no other island in the world.'

Off the western tip of the Island, the Needles have been a landmark for sailors for centuries. They stand sentinel to one of the most deadly stretches of water around the British coastline. And the sea is an ever-present force in the life of the Island – a contrast to the softness and greenery of much of its peaceful landscape.

Popular mythology has it that there is room for all the world's inhabitants on the Isle of Wight – if you allow one square foot per person. Such an invasion might not be welcomed by the average islander. For the people are private and protective of their boundaries, and not keen to mix it on the Mainland. It is a place of great physical beauty – rolling farmland, fertile pastures and sturdy manor houses.

TODAY, although the fishermen use outboard motors in their sleek, hand-built boats, there is still good work for sailmakers, who cater for the pleasure-boats and yachts, which have made the town of Cowes the most famous name in the boating world. One of these skilled and stalwart individualists is Hylton Mortimer, who has his sail loft in the river Yar Boatyard – just across the estuary from Yarmouth. Bright of eye and swift of hand, he is a craftsman of the old school. 'Just seeing all the big yachts come from Cowes up to Southampton when I was a boy made me want to take up making sails. Then I started my apprenticeship at Camper and Nicholsons more than thirty years ago. Had the good luck to work with some very good craftsmen. I suppose they've left a little of the skill behind. Most of them have gone now. . . . But then I decided that I'd like to go on my own here.'

Sitting in his modest shed, he reminds you of the pictures of the tailor of Gloucester as he tries to explain why people should come to him to have their sails made. 'I suppose the fact that I have very small premises means that I've got low overheads and so, of course, I'm more competitive. I do, in fact, still hand-finish sails because I haven't got the capital to invest in a lot of elaborate machinery, which modern sail-makers are now using. Being in that situation I do find it's better to carry on with traditional work. It does preserve it, and it's a better sail.'

As Hylton works, the huge sail crackles and rustles and billows around him. It feels as though you are in your sitting room with a semi-deflated barrage balloon. The work is accurate and detailed and meticulous and nothing is left to chance. 'The first principle – once you've taken the drawings from the sail plan or measured the spars of the yacht – is to have a large floor area to mark the sail out. Now I haven't got that. I just have the favour of being able to use the local Badminton Club, which has plenty of room, and, once the sail's set out and cut and marked up, I'm free of large rooms. Then I can carry on in this small place machining up and doing the hand-work. The hand-roping and, of course, working the bronze rings in by hand, instead of with the machine tool, takes a long time, but it's a superior job.'

T HE ancestors of men like Hylton Mortimer may well have made part of their living salvaging the wrecks, which were a commonplace on the dangerous shorelines of the Island 'back of the Wight'. It has always been a notoriously dangerous place for ships. And one of the busiest men on the Island is the Cox'n of the Yarmouth Lifeboat, Dave Kennett, who, with his crew, is on constant stand-by. Dark, tough and piratical, Dave pilots his cruelly fast boat through the roughest of seas and the strongest of currents, the hull almost hidden behind the huge bow-wave, which it pushes ahead of it. On board everything is trim, tidy and deadly efficient.

'I come from Freshwater Bay and, one way or another, I've been concerned with boats all my life. Started off with the few boats down there in the Bay and then graduated to trips round the Needles and operating down there, to eventually travelling round the world in the Merchant Service.

'In 1970 I took over as Cox'n. Being a Lifeboatman you have to change completely. You have to give up the travelling life. You have to establish yourself in a place like Yarmouth – and there's nothing finer than that. To my mind Yarmouth is one of the best places you could live. My whole life revolves round the lifeboat. I'm on call 24 hours a day and, apart from holidays when our second Cox'n takes over, I'm tied all the time.'

The chunky, brightly-coloured Lifeboat heads at speed for the Needles and, in the icy waters, a crewman in a life-jacket jumps overboard, so that a rescue can be practised in realistic conditions. An RAF helicopter is called in from Lee-on-Solent to help with the operation. 'We're very lucky on the Yarmouth Lifeboat. We've got a splendid crew. Seven in all – that's the Cox'n, second Cox'n, mechanic and assistant, and three crew members. We train every Sunday. Everything works well. The helicopter pilot understands exactly what we're doing. We have to lay into the wind 30 degrees off, so that he can fly into the wind and see the superstructure of the Lifeboat. Then the crewman can guide the winchman down onto the deck to pick up the rescued man and take him to hospital.

'One of our proudest rescues was in 1975 when we saved five London policemen. They had left Cherbourg in a south-easterly force 5 wind and were heading for the Needles when, about a mile offshore, the wind turned round to the north and blew about force 10. I'll always remember it. It was a terrible night, raining like anything; and it was very, very fortunate that these chaps had lots of red flares. We followed them and they were literally blown fifteen miles out into the Channel. We had a big sea running out there and we had to get alongside and take them off. Our mechanic, Bob Cook, at the time, he did quite a brave rescue by pulling a chap out of the sea over the side. Then we had to make our way back. We got a Silver Medal for that rescue.'

THE stretch of the Isle of Wight coast which has proved to be the most hazardous for shipping, is to the south-west of the island. The winds and waves lash this shoreline in foul weather, and the shallows are littered with wrecks. Paradoxically, if you travel east a few miles towards Ventnor, you come to the part of the island, which has, arguably, the most temperate and sheltered environment in the British Isles. As a result, plants, flowers and trees flourish here as nowhere else in the country. And this oasis of warmth is protected by the fact that, over the centuries, the cliff-face has slipped towards the sea creating an upper and an undercliff – the one protecting the other from the elements. Here, in the Ventnor area, bananas grow which would reach maturity if they were not picked too early by visitors; also dates, palm trees, cycads and a tropical jungle of exotic plants. It is a naturalist's paradise.

Even the less protected parts of the Isle of Wight, like Newtown, seem to enjoy a better climate than the mainland, and to produce their spring flowers, including the elegant, purple orchid, earlier and in greater profusion. And the red squirrels, of which the island is justly proud and protective, are an abiding delight to the local people and to the visitors.

Frank Heap of the National Trust takes a special pride in trying to encourage the growth of woodland flowers as he and his team of energetic volunteers revive the ancient skills of hedging and coppicing. The woods are carpeted with bluebells and the smoke from the fires, as the underbrush is cleared, mingles with the slim branches of the young trees in the pale sunlight.

'A copse is a small piece of woodland, which is cut regularly over a period of about eight years. Each time it's cut it grows up again – in fact, it grows up more densely than it did before. So it's a continually renewable resource that an ancient village would have relied on. And a small village, like Newtown, would have had a copse very similar to this, which most of its building materials, fire fuel and general home equipment would have been taken out of.'

Frank is a tall, gangling fellow, committed to his work and gentle with Nature. 'Already you can see a great bloom of bluebells and primroses, and the quicker we're out of the copse the better they'll do. So we try to move through as quickly as possible and with as little disturbance as we can.

'Since we've been cutting this area, we've begun to realise that it is an incredibly useful resource, even today. We've started to make hurdles. You begin with a board with holes in it, into which you put the vertical struts, which are made of split hazel. It's got to be slightly stouter stuff than the rest of the hurdle. Then, having split a large quantity of fairly thin hazel material – about an inch in diameter and preferably straight (that makes it a lot easier), you weave it in rather like basket-making. The trick is to be able to twist the ends in so that the whole hurdle is locked in and to end up with a hurdle with all the ends tied in as well, so that, when you pick the hurdle up, it doesn't fall apart.

'We've been fortunate enough to have folk who've worked on the land all their lives to come along and show us how it's done, and a variety of old crafts have come to light again, and we're trying our hand at them.'

DREDGING for oysters has probably been part of the way of life in the Isle of Wight as long as coppicing. It's almost certain that oysters were gathered here in Roman times. Today, oyster and clam farming is a busy, commercial enterprise, which, in the view of an experienced man like Derek Woodford, who earns his living from shellfish, still owes something to its ancient past. Even nowadays it can be a very tricky business. 'I do know that, apart from frost and too much fresh water in the river, shellfish – and oysters in particular – are prey to practically anything in the sea.

'You have to dredge the oysters and, in the life of an oyster, it is moved several times. As you grade them you find the smaller ones – not ready for eating yet – and they're put down in a separate bed and dredged in a year or two. When they've grown on to the right size – you keep your eye on them from time to time – they're taken to the shed and graded. Then we put them in trays in our tanks, where they're cleaned and they're ready for the market.'

It is an idyllic setting. The little dredger chugs out onto the calm estuary, and the water birds accompany it with their evocative calls. In the shed the shellfish rattle and snap as they roll through the grader and head for great swimming pools of clear water nearby. Derek Woodford is a serious and thoughtful man, every inch a seaman and full of knowledge about his trade.

'Clams, of course, are a different business. They come from Southampton Water where there's a lot of pollution. They're not graded or anything like that. They come straight from the fishing boats. They're put into this river in bags. Oh, they're very different from oysters. When they've done their stint in the river they're taken to the sheds and graded and then they go into the tanks as well – ready for market.'

He also rejects the claim that clams were introduced into this country from America. 'During our time working with clams we have found a fossilized clam, which is estimated to have been anything up to sixty million years old. That rather suggests that, if the Americans have given them to us in recent years, we gave 'em to them originally.'

IN the mouth of the river Yar, Andy Bird, slim, energetic and enthusiastic, runs a busy and successful fish market. The outside of his house is clad with hundreds of scallop shells and customers come from all over the Isle of Wight to buy fresh fish from him. 'The Island is fortunate. It's got some of the best lobster fishermen in England. Small boatmen too, like the Wheelers and the Blakes from Steephill Cove. They bring in beautiful stuff – you know, lovely local prawns, lobster, good crab. Oh yes, we've got some jolly good fishermen. But most of them are from around the 'back of the Wight' – from the Needles to St. Catherine's Point.

'Our crawfish we bring up from the West Country. You don't get many crawfish east of the Eddystone Light. They're mostly down the West Country – St. Ives Bay, the Isles of Scilly. We bring quite a number up each week and they sell quite well, although they're very dear. But when you get a good, big female with her eggs on her, why, they're better than caviar.'

Andy spends much of his time in the large tank inside his shop. Waders up to his thighs, he bends and seizes a great, struggling lobster from the depths. 'Well, that's a fine, great cob-lobster. He's probably been roaming round the sea-beds, I should think, for about eighteen years or more. Beautiful condition. Make a terrific meal. I suppose he's worth somewhere about £24. See his little swimming legs going there. Yeah, a very handsome fellow. I think this one was caught off the Needles somewhere. I've got two like it. I think they were both caught down off Scratchell's Bay.'

He reaches out for a vast tray of glowing pinks and greys and silvers – a fishy rainbow. 'Well, these are the prawns brought in from the Ventnor side of the Island by the Blakes and the Wheelers and, as you can see, they're beautiful, heavy, local prawns, all alive-o.' And Andy hurries on to the next customer and to the next load of fish.

THROUGHOUT the year the Isle of Wight is vibrant with birds, beasts, fish and flowers – all changing and competing with the seasons. But one of the most charming creatures you can see there seems unaffected by the time of year or by the changing temperatures. It is nothing but an ordinary, British donkey, submitting to the same task that donkeys have been performing in Carisbrooke Castle for nearly 300 years and probably much longer – pulling water by rope and wheel from a 160 foot well. It is not, of course, to provide the thirsty people of Carisbrooke with fresh water. But patiently to cater for the Isle of Wight's most valuable phenomenon – the tourist season.

SOUTHAMPTON WATER

SOUTHAMPTON Water, which feeds the famous, deep sea docks, is a mile wide and cuts ten miles into Southern Hampshire. The city, from which it takes its name, and the surrounding countryside, have, over the years, seen violent changes in fortune and appearance. It is not a place of tranquil beauty, though there are fascinating pockets of water birds and wildlife amidst the industrial scene. But it does have a dynamic and glamorous quality although, as the tides have ebbed and flowed over the centuries, the countryside has been attacked and invaded.

To the south is the Isle of Wight, protecting Southampton Water from the conflicting tides which swirl in from both east and west. In 1622 in *Polyolbion* Michael Drayton described it –

> 'And to the Northe, betwixt the fore-land and the firme,
> She hath that narrow sea, which we the Solent terme:
> Where those rough, ireful Tides, as in her Straits they meet,
> With boysterous shocks and rores each other rudely greet.
> Which fierclie when they charge, and sadlie make retreat,
> Upon the bulwarkt forts of Hurst and Calsheot beat,
> Then to southampton run.'

To the north, Southampton with its superb parkland still has much to recommend it, in spite of many ugly, new buildings; here the Test and the Itchen meet to form a straight and combined channel down to the Solent.

To the east, the river Hamble was once the centre of a busy, fishing industry. But now it is famous for leisure sailing. The fat cats in their gin palaces come and go. And many a juicy story for many a jaded gossip columnist has been observed and reported from these waters.

Westwards, the shore-line, known as the Waterside, is punctuated with power stations and chemical plants – vast, awe-inspiring blots on the landscape. But here, some last traces of what was the edge of the New Forest still fight for survival between the chimneys.

Ray Sedgewick operates a passenger ferry between Hamble village and Warsash. The ferry dates back as far as 1493, and still operates seven days a week.

ONE of the fine sights of Southampton is a toughly-built fishing boat heading out to sea in the dawn. The calm surface of the water breaks and reflects the early light, as the engine pushes it past factories and the main railway line towards the open sea. Like the men on board, the boat itself seems eager to reach the fresh air of the Channel away from the stink and sweat of industry and commerce. On the river Hamble, among the marinas and boatyards, crowded with pleasure craft and yachts, Jack Pallo is one of the few full-time fishermen left in the area. 'I started fishing with my father when I was nine years old. We used to fish out of here then. You had to have a permit, because it was during the war. I carried on part-time for years, first with my father and then on my own. And I suppose in 1968/69 I started to go full-time. Then I became so involved in fishing, I never done anything else.

'It's a close-knit community with the river people – the few that live on the river in boats, and those that make a living on the river. Then there's the people in the boatyards. And, of course, we get on well with them – if we spend money with 'em, they're going to look after us.'

Of course, Jack Pallo's lifestyle is very different from the way of life of the people on the big yachts, which are tied up close to his fishing boat. Jack is out often for 48 hours at a time – in all weathers and without sleep, while his neighbours are usually there for the easy life. But he does not seem to resent it.

'The Yacht Clubs in general – we manage very well with them. We don't have any friction anyway – not the friction that some people think there is between fishermen and yachtsmen. There's very little indeed, of course, even the yachtsmen have problems with the 'ooray 'Enrys, who come down from London and jump in a boat just as if they'd bought a car, and they shout and 'oller, "Get out of my way. You're across my bow" – and all this sort of rubbish. But that's a problem with individuals – not a problem with a class of people. And most of us know whose boat is which. We're all living in areas round Southampton Water, and every creek and inlet has got a fishing boat of some sort.'

Jack and his crew head West for a two day trip. The wind whips the surface of the water as the boat enters the Solent from the Hamble. The backdrop of Fawley Oil Refinery is like something out of a Science Fiction film. 'There's no easy living to be made out of the sea. On the other hand, it's not all that hard work.'

But there are many who work in the soft side of industry, who would find Jack's job physically impossible.

JUST below the place where Jack Pallo moors his boat, there is a passenger ferry between Hamble Village and Warsash. With his fiery red beard and sharp blue eyes, Ray Sedgewick rows his old boat backwards and forwards across the river, continuing a tradition that is more than 400 years old. If you travel with him, you don't just have a cheap ride. You also have the benefit of his easy conversation. It's a job that leaves his mind free for philosophy, and he is the friend and confidante of all those who regularly use the river.

'I've traced the history of the ferry back as far as 1493, but it's probably much older than that. The records are held in Winchester College and, unfortunately, before that date, they're written in mediaeval Latin, which is very difficult to get translated. The ferry operates seven days a week throughout the year. But not on Christmas Day. That's my official holiday. But I still come down and have a look to make sure everything is OK. Not many local people use it now. It's nearly all holiday people and children, who just like to come over and back for the ride.'

A distant figure waves from the far shore, and Ray clambers into the boat and rows off to pick up another fare. The busy river traffic crosses in front of him and behind, and his boat rocks and weaves in the wakes of the propellers as his oars pull him through the water.

To the north of Hamble, at Netley, there is a large area of meadowland and woods – a 280 acre park, which is a haven for wild life, with magnificent lawns reaching down to the water. Mature trees and wild flowers abound. Only twenty years ago, the Royal Victoria Hospital stood here – one of the grandest buildings of the 19th century. All that remains today is the domed chapel.

The hospital was built, with the support of Queen Victoria, to care for and cure the wounded soldiers coming home from the war in the Crimea. Florence Nightingale was not pleased with the facilities, but the building went ahead and many enjoyed its spacious beauty after the horrors of the war in Russia, though whether the echoing wards were much warmer than Crimean dug-outs is open to doubt.

It is unbelievable that even modern planners should have torn down such a magnificent building. But vanished it has – and forever – leaving a legacy of memories and the lovely Royal Victoria Country Park, where Ian Smith lives and works as the Head Ranger. For him the Park is a huge back garden.

'May's a good time of the year here – fresh greens on the trees and all the birds singing. We've just had a little drop of rain and the place is at its best, I think, in the springtime. The hospital was four hundred and some yards long – just over a quarter of a mile. It was the longest building in Europe when it was standing. It even beat the Palace at Versailles. There are stories that, during the Second World War, the Americans drove jeeps along the corridors when the hospital was in operation. I doubt that it's true, because I can't see the Matron at that time tolerating that sort of behaviour.'

Stories about the hospital are common. Everything about it was larger than life. At vast expense a jetty was built from in front of it straight out into Southampton Water, so that the troop ships, on their way home from Russia, could unload their wounded on the doorstep. After they had built for many months, they discovered that the water was too shallow for the ships to berth. Nobody had bothered to check the depth of the water before they began building the jetty.

Ian Smith can even tell a ghost story about the place. 'We've got a very nice legend with the hospital. We've got a resident ghost, which a lot of people have seen. She's called the Grey Lady. She is said to have fallen for one of the soldiers she was nursing and, with unrequited love, she leapt from one of the windows and killed herself. And I've been assured by several of the local people that she does walk about. So there are mysteries and surprises around every corner in this Country Park.'

Like everyone whose job is concerned with nature and wildlife, Ian is up early each morning. He is on duty all the time. But he would think more than twice before wanting to join the busy crowds of 9 to 5 workers in nearby Southampton.

Across the water at Hythe, passengers board a small train, which takes them half a mile across the shallows on a raised track to meet the ferry. This saves them a long and crowded journey by bus or car up the Waterside and into Southampton across the Test bridge. Directly opposite the Hythe Pier Terminal stands the

A tranquil stretch of the river Itchen near Eastleigh in Hampshire.

The tawny owl is the most common and widespread European owl. It is often found near human habitation, hunting in woods, parks and gardens, where its deep hooting call may be heard.

The river Hamble was once the centre of a busy fishing industry. It is now more famous for leisure sailing.

Drummond Arms Hotel – another pointer to the history of the Western Shore of Southampton Water. Two local landowners are brothers Maldwin and Bendor Drummond – whose Scottish ancestors ended up in Southern Hampshire after the '45 rebellion when the defeat of Bonnie Prince Charlie signalled the end of the clan system.

Nearby is a gracious folly overlooking the Solent and commanding spectacular views across to the Isle of Wight. 'Simon Lupton built his tower here in the early 18th century as a place for signalling to the smugglers at sea when to come in, and this would go on all the time. But poor, old Simon Lupton didn't make much out of it. He died in France, and Eaglehurst – as Lupton's Tower was called – was bought by a member of the aristocracy, who built the house, which is there now, in the form of a general's tent. The ceilings are just like a tent. When he died it was bought by the Drummonds to square off the Estate.'

The Drummond Estate is full of surprises. Near Fawley, Bendor Drummond has established a small, highly specialised business – a book bindery. Here, gold leaf, leather and skill combine to produce classic volumes of the old kind. 'Well, I was reading *Country Life* one day and there was a book review about how you could bind books yourself. I had the idea that you could – rather like girls do tatting – do it on your lap while you were looking at television or listening to the radio or a bit of music, and that you could just sew it on like that. A friend of mine, who'd gone through a book binding course, suddenly said to me that there was one available at Southampton College of Art. So I went along and learned and I found out that you couldn't do it on your lap at all. It was really quite complicated. When some offices, which used to be the Estate Offices for Cadland Estate, became available, I decided I'd love to make a bindery and my partner and I started this together.'

ONLY ten minutes drive from Southampton Water is the village of Exbury and Exbury Gardens – a magnificent plantation of rhododendrons, azaleas and camelias. In the spring the colours are overwhelming in their richness and variety. The head gardener at Exbury is Doug Betteridge, who has worked on the Estate for more than thirty years. A major part of his work is the creation of new species. 'There is always something to try to achieve in terms of colour or length of flowering or a compact truss. There's always a specific end result that we are aiming for. But some of our flowers we're never going to improve. Even with hybridisation there are one or two, which are so beautiful, that we'll never make them any better. Our main flowering period lasts about four months. May is the best time to come, but there's always something in flower.'

The careful tending of this great 260 acre garden over the years has made it the crowning glory of the countryside around Southampton Water.

NOWADAYS there are many people who see the loss of passenger traffic to the aeroplane as a death-blow to the heart of Southampton, where industries, communities and buildings have flourished and passed into oblivion with unsettling haste. But the unique geographical features of the area ensure its survival as a changing and exciting part of the English landscape.

WATERSHIP DOWN

IF Richard Adams had not written his famous rabbit adventure, Watership Down would still just be the attractive name of an unknown, Hampshire hill. Today the rabbits still abound, and the tourists have come flocking in to visit the scenes of their wars and travels. In some ways this has brought unwanted pressure onto these gentle, Hampshire uplands. Lovers have carved their names on the handsome beech trees, and some of the more obvious paths and tracks are well worn and scarred with litter. But, away from the main roads, the countryside is still quiet and fertile and unchanged. And the river Test, which flows through the area, is as clear and sparkling as crystal, and is arguably this country's number one trout stream, though there are many who cannot afford to fish it. Here too are some of Britain's finest and most prosperous cereal farmers with spacious fields and generous soils.

William Cobbett came to Watership Down over 150 years ago and rode over 'the North Hampshire hills, which, notwithstanding their everlasting flints, I like very much. As you ride along, even in a green lane, the horse's feet make a noise like hammering. It seems as if you were riding on a mass of iron. Yet the soil is good and bears some of the best wheat in England. All these high and indeed all chalky lands are excellent for sheep. But, on the top of some of these hills, there are as fine meadows as I ever saw. Pasture richer perhaps than that about Swindon in the north of Wiltshire. And the singularity is that this pasture is on the very tops of these lofty hills, from which you can see the Isle of Wight. Though the grass grows finely, there is no apparent wetness in the land. The wells are more than three hundred feet deep. The main part of the water for all uses comes from the clouds, and indeed these are pretty constant companions of these chalk hills . . .'

IT would be disappointing to visit the area around Watership Down without finding some rabbits. If you take the small, winding back road from Whitchurch and can spare a moment to stop from time to time on the way to the Downs, you are certain to see rabbits by the hedges, basking in the sun or playing in the shady lanes.

If rabbit-watching is too much trouble for you, Bridget Dodman keeps and breeds scores of them at the Watership Down Inn at Freefolk. But they are rather different from Hazel and Fiver and Bigwig. 'When I started to collect rabbits, I decided to go in for the more unusual ones – Angoras, Himalayans and that sort of thing. Then,

Watership Down, the north Hampshire area now more well-known as the site of Richard Adams' novel of the same name.

when I saw my first English Lop, I started showing them, and that's what started the whole thing off.'

Bridget produces a large bundle of white, woolly fur. It might be a large cat or a small sheep, which had missed a season's shearing. If you look carefully, though, you will find some ears, which look suspiciously like those of a rabbit. 'He's an Angora — what they call a fancy rabbit. I'm quite used to them, but it's surprising how many people have never seen one. He's just a domestic rabbit. They're not quite sure how they came about. But he is for show and his lovely coat is a wool and can be spun for knitting.'

As Bridget moves along the scores of cages in her garden shed feeding the rabbits

32

and checking their water a head pops out of one of the little doors. The ears are so long that they hang a good two or three inches below the floor-level of the cage as the head peeps out. 'This one is an English Lop. His ears are purely for show, I'm afraid, though they are amazingly warm to the touch on a chilly day. He doesn't really suffer with them, except that sometimes he trips over them.'

Further down the line three delightful young rabbits share a home together. They are small and neat and perfect, and they are coloured black and white or brown and white. They are Dutch rabbits – everyone's ideal of what a pet rabbit should be.

Sitting on a straw-bale outside her rabbit hotel, Bridget talks of how local friends and neighbours bring green food to the pub for her hungry hordes. She is slim and pretty with high cheekbones and hair that shines even more than the coat of the small grey Netherland Dwarf rabbit that sits happily on her knee.

IN 1877 the son of Charles Dickens described this part of Hampshire as being 'surrounded by smiling farms and watered by one of those clear and fresh rivulets of troutful water, accounted among the chief commodities of Hampshire'. Barry and Ann North live close to the river Test at Tufton. When he is not busy farming, Barry finds time to cut sedge from the riverside for Ann to plait and weave into beautiful baskets and carriers.

It is a superb setting. The smooth river runs through rough woodland. Young swans swing in overhead to practise landing on the flat surface of the water. Coots and moorhens scamper for safety and Barry, waders up to his thighs and sickle in his right hand, strides across the river towards the far bank. 'Once it dies off, the sedge is burnt in early spring. About March time. That's the natural way of keeping it down. I just cut enough sedge for my wife to make the baskets. I take it home and hang it up to dry – very much like a farmer does hay. Once it's dried then it's fit to use. It's a very old craft, taught to my wife by the gamekeeper's wife and Ann does it now because she wants to keep the skill alive.'

In a magnificent, thatched Tudor barn with tall doors reaching up to the roofline and a golden mountain of wheat stored on the floor, Ann North stands to plait the sedge and to make her delicate creations. The beams inside the barn have been shaped by craftsmen out of solid oak trees, and sparrows flicker between them as they help themselves to their share of the harvest. Tied high on one of the old walls is a row of tidy bundles of dried sedge, awaiting Ann's strong and skilful hands.

'There's lots of colours in it – pinks and greens and browns. Once the sedge has matured you lose the other colours and it becomes almost gold. If you put it out in the bright sunlight you lose all the colour. It just bleaches. So you need to keep the bundles in the dark to dry for about three weeks to set the colours. Each of the little sheafs that we tie it into for drying will make about a yard of finished material and will take about an hour to plait. So basically all I'm doing is seven strand plaiting.'

But the work is meticulous and even and demands both patience and concentration. 'If you're making something heavy like a log basket you create much thicker plaits, using a lot more sedge in each one. If you're just doing a small shopping basket then you don't make it quite so thick. You do a finer plait.' Ann works on through the morning, and her skill and industry are confirmed by the high quality of what she produces and the speed with which the baskets roll off her one-woman assembly line.

A FEW miles North of Whitchurch on the road to Newbury lie the wide acres of one of the best-known Hampshire farmers, Lord Porchester. His land stretches out from Beacon Hill towards Watership Down. Kestrels hover overhead and a stoat bounces and bounds through the tussocks in search of food.

On the steep journey down from Beacon Hill Lord Porchester, who is, of course, one of the great breeders of great race-horses, stops to admire distant groups of aristocratic creatures in the meadows and paddocks of his Highclere Stud.

'It is a most beautiful place. On a clear day you can see seven counties from up here. We're so lucky having the variation of soils so close to one another. And the natural lie of the land helps the crops. The barley is earlier on the south facing fields than on the other ones.

'Like the barley, the horses also benefit from the sun. So that's why all our yards are facing South. I've been steeped in breeding them from my boyhood, and I've always been very interested in pedigrees and matings.'

The Stud is immaculate. The buildings are clean and tidy. The grass is perfect. Up a long, metalled road a group of grooms is leading a string of magnificent breeding mares. In front of a block of stables a big, grey horse is being schooled on a long rein. And the colts and yearlings scamper and squabble as they are fed deep in a sun-drenched meadow.

'We try and treat them all the same and we hope we manage them well. They're cosseted to the extent of being well fed and well looked after. Because one animal is more valuable than another one, in terms of the nomination fee, it doesn't follow that we give it any more attention than one that is less valuable. In fact, that approach can be counter-productive. You can worry so much about the price of a horse that it makes it more likely that you will make mistakes. We simply aim to give them all first-class treatment. I don't really allow myself to have favourites but, if I had to choose, I'd say that *Silk Stocking*, who has that lovely *Mill Reef* colt foal, is one of my favourite mares and, of course, old *JoJo*, who is the dam of many of my fillies and the grandmother of *Little Wolf*, who won the Ascot Gold Cup, is another.'

The pride of the stud at Highclere is *Teenoso*, a black stallion with gleaming coat and rippling muscles, which look like mighty steel cords and plates under the glossy skin. He has whiplash reactions and a highly bred disdain for the rest of the world. He makes Black Beauty or the Lloyds Bank horse look like old has-beens.

I N an area which is dominated by the river Test, head river-keeper David Walford from beautiful Bere Mill has a busy time keeping the river clean and tidy and looking after the fish. He and his colleagues are often hard at work wading through the water and keeping the weed growth down with wicked-looking scythes. 'I've always been interested in fishing and country life, and this is the kind of job I always wanted to do. People often say that we're cutting weeds. But I like to call them river plants. The growth in the upper waters of the Test is very heavy and we have four, individual cuts during the season. In the autumn we just cut but, at the other times, we also rake the gravel in the shallows and make little lays for the spawning fish. We also trim the margins of the river banks towards the end of the year to make it neat and tidy. That gives everything a clean start from May 1st of the following year when the season starts.'

Almost all the fish in the Test are wild trout and David Walford sometimes finds the time to try and catch some of them himself. More often though you will find him up to his elbows in water, clad in a huge, black rubber apron, grading rainbow trout at the fish farm nearby. Long rectangles of black water, guarded by barbed wire and ferocious Alsatian dogs, are the homes for tens of thousands of fat fish. If you stand at the edge and throw in some food pellets the placid surface turns in an instant into a boiling cauldron of hungry trout.

'At the hatchery we strip our own eggs from the mature fish. We grow those on into fingerlings and then into adults. We're trying to provide a good quality stock of trout, which we then sell to other river-bank owners. I can't say that there isn't a tame fish in our water, but we try very hard to keep our own fishing private and stocked with wild ones.'

Close to the mill is an eel trap. It is a pit and a grille, through which all the river water can be made to pass. At the right time, the bottom of the well is a squirming mass of shiny eels and David, clad as usual in waders and waterproofs, scoops them up in scores into a plastic bin. 'Eels are a seasonal thing – what we call a catch crop. They come up into the fresh water to grow. We set our trap, normally in what is called a dark period or when there is a waning moon, and we catch these mature eels going back to the sea. We don't get that many 'cos we're right at the top of the river. But they're a delicacy and we sell a few to people from Billingsgate, and some we have smoked and we eat them ourselves.'

As David Walford surveys the river, the fine, old, yellow mill, the serenity of the overhanging trees and the charming, redbrick, hump-backed bridge, which carries the road over the Test to his home, he seems contented with his lot.

IN Whitchurch James Potter is keeping alive one of the oldest skills in the world with the talented help of his son and grandson. Apprenticed in 1926 he has been for sixty years an expert and artistic silversmith.

The silver gleams in the bow window of the shop in Newbury Road. Every kind of cutlery, cup, mug and jewellery is there. The workshop behind is a hive of activity. Molten lead is poured into moulds, silver spoons are hammered and shaped, patterns are chiselled, polishers whirl, and gas flames roar as the silver is softened. 'Hand forging isn't much done these days. There are still some who do it — I'm not the only one — but the thing is it's a time-wasting process. And people are all for speed these days. So they use blanks. And all you've got to do then is to decorate them. There's no real hand-mades that goes into the modern stuff. But it's what people can afford. And I must be honest with you, it's not quite as good. But it looks as good. With hand-forging the silver is a lot tougher and it wears well.'

While James Potter talks, his son (who left the police to join his father) and his grandson are hard at work. Both men have learnt their skills from a master craftsman. 'I got so busy after I started on my own that I didn't know where all the

James Potter keeps one of the oldest skills in the world alive in his workshop at Whitchurch. He has been for sixty years an expert and artistic silversmith.

people were coming from. I was snowed under with work, so I took on my son. I let him know that the opportunity was there for him. But I never asked him. He asked me, because I thought that it can be a little bit difficult picking a secure career like the Police Force and then becoming a Silversmith, where the work can fluctuate. So, in the end, he decided to come, which pleased me a lot, because it took a load off my shoulders. Also he brought his son into it with him. And now my grandson's made some nice, little individual pieces. He's very skilful, I think, so we've got the three generations. It pleases me because I know we're going to have the continuity, and it's an old craft that's being kept alive all the time.'

THERE is still much to admire and learn from in this small piece of the heart of Hampshire, and Edward Thomas wrote a powerful description of it in his book, *The South Country*:

'Yet another frost follows, and in the dim, golden light just after sunrise, the shadows of all the beeches lie on the slopes, dark and more tangible than the trees, as if they were real and those standing upright were the returned spirits above the dead. Now rain falls and relents and falls again all day, and the earth is hidden under it and, as from a land submerged, the songs mount through the veil. The mists waver out of the beeches like puffs of smoke or hang upon them or in them like fleeces caught in thorns. In the just penetrating sunlight the long boles of the beeches shine, and the chaffinch, the yellowhammer and the cirl bunting sing songs of blissful drowsiness. The Downs, not yet green, rise far off and look, through the rain, like old thatched houses.'

BEAMINSTER

IF you travel to the West Country in the summer, you are likely to be besieged and surrounded by caravans, campers and pleasure-hunters. Devon, Dorset, Somerset and Cornwall are clogged with canvas and beset by traffic jams. An oasis of pastoral peace in this strident holiday world is Beaminster in West Dorset. It is a small, country town, set in a bowl of hills and steep banks – the kind of place about which Thomas Hardy wrote with such love and accuracy. Here is some of the most beautiful scenery in Britain. Described once as 'the forgotten county', Dorset has benefited from its lack of sex-appeal and – inland at least – remains largely unspoilt and free from the blinkered gaze of tourism.

Beaminster itself is first recorded as Bebingmynster in 872 A.D. But burial grounds in the surrounding, wooded hills – famous for sheltering the elusive Roe deer – date back to prehistoric times. Devastated by fire in 1644, 1684 and 1781, Beaminster has always recovered, and it stands today as solid and respectable as a Victorian nursemaid – and even more attractive.

Like every town and village in the country, Beaminster's war memorial bears witness to the sacrifice of many of its sons in the conflicts of the twentieth century. Above the town in a private place on a hill-top, watched over by butterflies and hovering hawks, is another simple grave-stone commemorating a remarkable father and son, who could never have known one another. The father died winning the first-ever airforce VC in the War to end all Wars. His pilot son died winning the DFC in the war which followed it.

STONE from the surrounding oolitic hills has gone into the building of many of Beaminster's fine, old houses with their mellow, honey-coloured walls. They date back two, three and even four hundred years. Scores of skilled stone-masons used to earn a good living in the area. Today the numbers have dwindled dramatically. But men like John Page still build and repair houses and churches with the same craftsmanship and artistry, which have been handed down over the centuries.

'It's an art in itself. You've got to know the stone – the grain of the stone – before you can lay it. There's no good laying the stone the wrong way up. Otherwise, after a few years, it just falls apart. Unfortunately, most of the quarries these days aren't worked, so most of the stone that we use is second-hand. Sometimes an old cottage is being pulled down and the local builder buys the stone, and then we re-use it.'

Not far from the town stands a magnificent, thatched farm-house. At one end, the stone and the roof are weathered and graceful. At the other end, the walls are brand new and the roof unmarked. But the style and the feel of the old building have been retained, and it is possible to see that, after a few decades of wind and weather, the match will be nearly perfect. This work is one of John Page's proudest achievements.

'This place is a classic example of a modern stonemason's job at its best. The old house was struck by lightning. In fact, we could see it from our kitchen window. We could actually see the flames come up over the top of the hill. We saw the red glow when the roof went in, and we could see all the sparks going up in the air. It was fantastic. And, of course, the next day we came up and had a look at it, and it was devastating really. So we went to work and this is the result. We're all quite proud of it.'

John is a short, dark man. His face is as weathered by the Dorset sun, wind and rain as the stone, on which he works his magic. 'I took a five year apprenticeship with the local firm, because opportunities for work aren't great in rural districts. I thought to myself, "Well, it's a nice life to get outside in the sunshine." I was right about the sunshine, but it's not so funny in the winter. Anyway, I served my apprenticeship and I was lucky that I worked on about eight houses during that time. You know, stone, brick and reconstructed stone. But the best ones is stone ones — absolutely marvellous.'

John is enthusiastic about his home town. 'This is a good place for a stone-mason, because one gets a variety of jobs. You might be doing a stone wall one day, and then, the following week, you could be building a house or working on the Church — or anywhere around the district. Not necessarily in Beaminster itself. Of course, a lot of the Churches are getting old like everything else and they need renovating quite a lot.'

THERE seems to be a genuine community spirit in Beaminster, although some local people say that it has diminished with the influx of outsiders over the last couple of decades. The cricket team plays well and frequently and the visitors come from far afield. Regular opponents are the Wye Rustics from Kent. Beaminster loyalist and stalwart of their cricketers is their wicket-keeper and opening batsman, Maurice Hannam. He's a florid, cheerful man with a greeting for everyone as he walks through the town.

'Summer is very special to me. You've just got to look around the area here and you can see everything you want. I'm a country boy at heart. I've always lived in the country. Nearly every Sunday afternoon — particularly in the winter — I go out walking regardless of the weather. I put on me wellies and waterproofs and walk all up across the hills. And it's a wonderful experience, even when it's raining. You let the elements hit your face and it's very refreshing.'

The sun shines. The Church bell tolls eleven. The cricketers come out of the pavilion whirling their arms round their heads, and jigging up and down to calm their nerves. 'We're not too bad. We used to do very well ten years ago when three of us in the side played for the County. It's not as good now. We've got some youngsters coming on, but they tend not to play too much when they leave school these days. You've just got to get them from where you can. When you play in the strongest league in the County, you've got to compete in places like Dorchester and Weymouth. I mean Weymouth is 26,000 people or something like that. This is only 2,300. We go to Bournemouth and Poole – that's big competition, you know. But we've done very well, really. We've won the Championship twice – in '72 and '74. We've been runner up five times. So, all in all, we've done pretty well.'

During the lunch-break some of the cricketers and their supporters head for the Sun Inn in East Street for a few sharpeners and a bit of gossip. Back at the cricket, Maurice Hannam sits on a grass bank in the afternoon sunshine and remembers games gone by. 'When we used to play in the village knock-out competition four or five years ago, we were playing Kingston Lacey in the final. They wanted 24 to win with four wickets left. They were going well. They virtually had the game sewn up. Then this chappy hit the ball to mid-wicket or mid-on – somewhere out there. I was keeping wicket at the time. Meantime, these two were running up and down. I could hear them thumping and banging about. Anyway, at last the ball came in to me at the stumps and I knocked the bails off. Unknown to me, when I looked round, these two lads had obviously collided. Actually, one had hit the other one on the head with a bat 'andle by mistake. They were both looking at the ball and they just ran into one another. One was run out by me. The other one was knocked out up the other end of the wicket. He looked a sorry sight and was unconscious. We phoned for a doctor. We called him the local horse doctor. His comment, when he saw the injured man, was, "That's all right. I'll stitch him up and put him in the stable with a bale of hay and he'll be as right as ninepence." Well, all in all, it was quite a good day, because we won the game as well.'

During the tea interval players, girl-friends and wives sit in groups round the pavilion. The conversation is desultory. The spectators feed their picnics to their dogs – too hot to feel hungry themselves, and small children scamper. Maurice Hannam remembers another epic Beaminster match.

'Several years ago, we were playing against Taunton St. Andrews. They were a very nice bunch of fellows. Good socialisers. They were fielding. A neighbour living beside the cricket ground used to keep bees. It was a hot day, very close, a bit like today. And all these bees came over in a big swarm. As they came across the ground everyone was diving for it. You could see all the blokes lying down one at a time as the swarm came across. After the bees had gone, everyone finally stood up. But there were still bees about and people were stung on heads, noses, legs, arms, everywhere. Helluva state it was. And afterwards everyone was wearing caps. And that's most unusual to find eleven people in a field wearing caps, you know. That was a pretty grim day for the visitors really, because they were in a bit of a state – lumps all over the place.'

DOMINATING the town is the lovely, old Church of St. Mary. In Anglo-Saxon the name, Beaminster, translates as 'Church among the trees'. Maurice Hymas is one of the local butchers. With his impressive band of bell-ringers of all ages, he is helping to keep alive another of those important skills, which technology is doing its utmost to destroy.

'We've got eighteen qualified ringers and we've got about five youngsters that are beginners. They started by ringing hand-bells with one of our senior ringers. Bell-ringing is like riding a bicycle really. It takes some time and it is a job you have to take seriously. You should start off by getting used to handling the rope.'

High in the bell-tower the ringers show the newcomers how it's done. In the belfry above, the huge bells swing and rock and tumble, and the tower shakes and trembles as the peels ring out across the summer meadows. When the learners start to practise, Maurice Hymas takes pity on the local population. 'Normally we tie the clapper up – that's the metal inside the bell, which strikes the inside of the bell. We fasten it so that we're not causing a nuisance to the people living round the church. It's an annoying sound one bell just going 'doing, doing, doing.' So you can get the learners to practise without causing any disturbance and, of course, that improves their ringing. The hard physical work is really just in raising the bells. Once the bells are raised for ringing, it's quite easy because they are all finely balanced.'

ON a summer evening, Beaminster doctor's son, Simon Horner, enjoys the distant sound of the Church bells across the fields. But he prefers fishing for fat, brown trout in a local lake, where the trees and the setting sun combine to make breath-taking reflections.

'This is a convenient place because it's close to home and the fish are large. There are also a lot of them, which makes it easier to catch them. People say that lake fishing is very simple, but you've still got to present the fly in the correct way for a fish to take it. They're stocked once a year and they vary in size from about 3 pounds up to 7 or 8 pounds. So you could have quite a battle on your hands when you hook one.'

A handsome 4 pound fish is landed after a ten minute struggle and Simon reluctantly interrupts his fishing to talk again. 'Fishermen have theories about everything, especially the weather. As far as I'm concerned it's not so likely that I'll catch a fish if there's very bright sunlight. And, if it's raining, it's not so likely. But, generally speaking, I hope to get one or perhaps two. If they're four or five pounds, it's quite enough for a while. It's the family well fed.' And he turns back to his rod and the lake and more serious matters.

THE wild hedges around the small Dorset fields and along the steep banks make a perfect foraging ground for honey-bees. As a result, there are many people in Beaminster who make fine Dorset honey for both pleasure and profit. Clad in her white, protective uniform and green veil, Joan Passage from Netherbury is one of the enthusiasts. 'You can tell by tasting the honey where the bees have been working. Around here our main crop comes from blackberries. That means that our honey comes in rather later than in some parts of the country.'

As the bees, heavy with pollen, pour into the hives from the nearby woods and heathland, some of them begin to perform their famous dance. 'They manage to tell each other about finding a new source of nectar by doing a sort of figure-of-eight movement on the comb inside the hive. The size of the loop, which they make, indicates the distance away of the new type of flower. It tells the other bees how far they have to go. And the polarised light as it reflects on the entrance of the hive, together with the magnetism of north, shows the bees where to fly to find the new crop. Some bees search these crops out. Others just work them.

'We don't take our honey until early August – then it's ready for our local show at the end of August. In July we hope to be adding new supers to the hives. That means that we put another layer on the top of the hive above the bees where they're working, so that they have more room and can increase their production of honey and nectar.'

PARTICULARLY in the summer months, Beaminster is the antidote to the rat-race. It incorporates everything which modern man seems determined to destroy – tranquillity, peace, beauty and great richness of wild-life. Like many isolated country areas it is cold and bleak in the winter. But the glory of the spring, summer and autumn more than compensate for the discomfort of winter. If Dorset is indeed the forgotten county, it has not been forgotten in vain.

PORTLAND

THOMAS Hardy described Portland as 'The Gibraltar of Wessex' and he wrote, 'It stretches out like the claw of a bird into the English Channel. The towering rock, the houses above houses – one man's doorstep rising behind his neighbour's chimney; gardens hung up by one edge to the sky, the vegetables growing on apparently vertical planes, the unity of the whole Island as a solid and single block of limestone four miles long.'

Portland would be an island today if it was not for the capricious tides, which have, over the centuries, heaped a giant, twelve-mile ridge of pebbles between it and the mainland. This is the mighty Chesil Beach, and it runs from Portland to Bridport. The stones on the beach vary in size, depending on how far you are from Portland. Local fishermen claim that, in fog, they can tell their position precisely when they ground their boats by the size of the pebbles under their boots.

The Island's name is said to come from a Saxon pirate called Port, who captured it in 501 A.D. The Romans called it Vindillis, and archaeologists have discovered many traces of the Roman occupation. But the earliest inhabitants were probably a race of Spanish or Portuguese nomads, called Iberians, who wandered across Britain in pre-Roman times.

Portland is renowned for its bird-life. The rocky cliff-faces provide a perfect haven for every kind of seabird. In the spring it is the arrival point in England for many migrating birds, tired after the long sea-crossing. And, although the Island is virtually bare of trees, it still has an abundance of plants and flowers and butterflies. Above all, it boasts with pride some of the finest views in the British Isles – east towards the Isle of Wight and west towards Land's End.

The Island is justly famous for its stone, its quarries and its houses. Many fortunate, fine buildings are made of Portland stone. Perhaps the best known is St. Paul's Cathedral. Even today, the occasional block of stone bearing Sir Christopher Wren's personal wine-glass mark lies unused on the sea-shore or in some long-abandoned quarry. And the massive breakwater was built of local stone by the inmates of Portland Prison, which was established in 1848 when the Australians began to protest about the number of new convicts still being dumped on their shores from the old country.

Traditionally, the people of Portland are private and insular. Mainlanders are contemptuously called Kimberlins or Foreigners. Today, although thousands cross the causeway to and from work and holiday-makers galore crowd in to enjoy the spectacular views and the sea air, there is still a deep-rooted suspicion of outsiders and their ways.

FISHING has always been one of Portland's main industries. The waters are deep and dangerous, but the catches can be good. There are far less lobsters than of old because of over-fishing, but there is still an abundance of crabs for skilled men like Derek Galpin. With his red face and sturdy figure, he is every inch a fisherman, and he launches his sharp-prowed boat from the steeply-banked and rounded stones of the Chesil beach as if it was sliding into the water on wheels.

'I've lived in Portland all me life. I just don't want to shift now. The fishing used to be very good. But it's getting worse every year. Even the crabs are getting less. There's just too many people fishing for them. Because of unemployment you've got a lot of men around the coast here with time on their hands. We've got the Jersey boats and the French boats. Some of them take the lobsters when they're smaller

Portland, the 'Gibraltar of Wessex', would be an island were it not for the twelve mile ridge of pebbles known as the Chesil Beach between it and the mainland.

Portland Bill is one of the nation's beauty spots. The lighthouse warns shipping not only of the cruel rocks, but of the Race where several tides meet. The whirlpool created there has caused the death of many fine ships.

45

Bluebells present a lovely sight in woods and hedgerows during springtime. Their survival in the wild is still threatened by people who tread on them whilst picking their flowers. Fortunately it is now illegal to dig up the bulbs, though curiously these used to be dug for use in making starch for clothing.

than they should be. It takes lobsters and crabs a long time to grow – ten years for a lobster and six years for a crab. A lobster gets up to about 8 or 9 pounds, and then it don't get any bigger. But most of the big ones have been caught now.'

The small outboard engine drives the heavy, wooden boat along the edge of Portland towards Portland Bill. The cries of the seabirds – gulls, puffins, guillemots – echo off the cliff-faces as Derek and his mate haul in their pots, empty them, re-bait them and lower them back into the deep. Today there are several pots with nothing in them. 'Yes, the fishing is getting poorer and poorer. Plus the price don't go up. It's the same price as it was ten years ago. But the cost of everything else goes up. It's a good life though, you know. You're your own boss.'

The waters around Portland can be savage in the wild weather. The cliffs and rocks – many hidden close beneath the surface – are formed of the same stone which has served St. Paul's so well. They can tear the bottom out of a fishing boat in a second. Derek Galpin, who works from dawn to dusk in conditions which would turn away most modern workers, is philosophical about the difficulties. 'Oh, you just take the weather as it comes. If it's bad, you can't fish. You've got to stay ashore and repair your pots. But you have to go out every day it's possible in order to make a living. The other side of that is that you get more crabs when the water's thick after rough weather, because what they feed on is moving about on the bottom. The crabs really start moving then.

'October is the worst month because the crabs gotta go out and feed more. They get soft – what we call shy. They change their shells and then come back in again – a size bigger. They've gotta be 5½ inches across before you can keep 'em.'

Back on shore, strong, reticent women cook the crabs and tear them apart before packing them up, ready for their journey to the markets. Derek is proud of the quality of the fish he catches. 'Through the years it's always been renowned that Portland crabs are the best. It's the rocky bottom, I think – and all these big ledges. They've got to be good condition crabs to live in this, when you get a south-westerly gale. They sell some of 'em locally, but mostly they go to London.' Derek's boat heads off round Portland Bill in search of more delicacies for the wealthy gourmets in London's West End.

BEFORE the ferry bridge opened, Portlanders were even more cut off than they are today, and rarely married outsiders. There were just a few local names, and most people were given nicknames in order to distinguish them. Two loyal islanders, who married recently, are Julie Sellen and Steven Browne, who works as a fishmonger in a rickety stall just before the road to Portland starts its steep and winding climb up the cliff. With his dark hair and quick smile you can see traces of those ancient Iberian nomads in his features. And the quality and variety of the fish he sells would do credit to the smartest London fish shop.

'This is a strange, old island. Very few families on it are genuine Portlanders – only two or three really. We young 'uns don't really worry about things like that any more – whether we marry a Portland girl or an outsider. It's a pity in a way. It's only the older hands who are concerned about it nowadays.'

Steven is predictably proud of Julie. She is fair, open-faced and full of vigour. 'She's very quiet and very tiny. We met at the local Carnival dance. She was one of the Carnival Queen's attendants, and I went up there and just got to know her. It was a quick relationship – just two or three years – and then we married. I didn't think it was going to come so quick.'

But his attitude to his new, young wife might not go down quite so well in those places where feminism reigns. 'She's always at home. Gets the grub when I get home an' that. She's very good she is. Does the ironin' without even being asked. When we bought this house, I had to live here for seven months on me own until we got married. She wouldn't move in. You know, she had her principles and that was that. But I'm glad she's there now. Because, when you go home at night-time after a 'ard day, you've got somebody to look after you – and that's the main thing. Otherwise it's a bit lonely. I was in a family of nine and, when you live on your own for seven months, it drives you up the wall.

'I've only got one criticism of Julie – she doesn't like fish at all. But she doesn't mind the job. She even comes with me on long journeys like up to London and the fish farm – in spite of the smell in the van.'

With his broad Dorset accent veteran Portland poet, George Davey, recalls some of the Islanders' less conventional marriage customs. 'Years ago it was the fashion for a young man and a woman on Portland to get together and, if the man's seeds were fertile, well, then they'd get married. But if 'is seeds fell on stony ground, well, then it was quite all right for 'im to leave the one that he was courtin' and go and cast his seeds elsewhere. And then, should that be fruitful, well, then they would get married.'

Julie Sellen is not too sure about some of the old customs, but her loyalty to the Island itself is unbending. 'We'll never leave Portland. Never. It's one place that, if you move there, you never really want to leave again. Portland's a place you can never stay away from; the people – everyone – they're so friendly. You know practically everybody where it's such a small place. It's just great. We'll never leave here. Never.'

Portland stone was originally carved out of the cliffs of the Island and was transported by horsedrawn railway and ship. Constant quarrying since the Middle Ages has ravaged much of the land and has left it a fascinating moonscape. The strength and skills of today's quarrymen, like Ralph Stone, are no less than those of their predecessors. But modern machinery had speeded things up and has made it possible for outsiders to comprehend how those massive blocks of stone can be handled.

'The quarry I'm working at the moment must 'ave been dug over a period of about forty years, I should imagine. It's a luxury sort of building stone. It really is. I don't

Stephen Browne works as a fishmonger in his native Portland, where his family have lived for generations.

know if people could afford to have a building built of solid Portland stone any more.'

The crane bangs and jerks as mighty segments of honey-coloured stone are levered free. Wielding his heavy power drill Ralph stands on the brink of a sheer, 100 foot drop, apparently unconcerned by the potential for death and destruction on every side of him. His eager Jack Russell terrier quivers with excitement as the stones are lifted. He's expecting to see a rabbit bolt from underneath the huge blocks. 'It's all full of joints you know. It may look pretty solid to you. But it's all in pieces. Some of them are big. Some are small. And you just have to attack it as you see fit. We're looking to produce 200 metres a month. We can earn a good wage on that. One metre of stone weighs about 2½ tons. We have quarried great, big stones for special customers. About 6 or 7 metres we've 'ad 'em. Special cranes for lifting them and all sorts of stuff like. But this old crane 'ere will only pick up about 24 ton as he is now.'

Ralph and his mates take one of the rubber pipes from the compressor, which drives the drills, and use the air, which screams out under pressure, to blow the dust from their muscled bodies. They are built like weight-lifters. As they clean up, the terrier seizes the rubber pipe as it thrashes about and worries it furiously – like a mongoose with a cobra. 'All the quarrying in the old days was done from landslides of rock around the cliffs. What fell down years ago, the quarrymen went along and picked it up. It weren't no quarrying like we're doing now. Just picking up all the bits and pieces that fell over, shaping it up and chucking it in the barges in the water, see. Then taking it up to London out of the way.'

In the distance the vast and forbidding walls of Portland Prison shimmer in the summer heat. No chance there of cutting a way out through the formidable stone, and Ralph is certain of the quality of his product. 'It's not really attacked by the weather that much. You can just cut it back an eighth of an inch and you've got a brand new lump of stone again. It's pretty impervious to the weather or the atmosphere or one thing an' t'other. People talk about reinforced concrete. A disaster, weren't it? You see all those tower blocks falling down. Portland stone just doesn't deteriorate like it. I know it's more expensive to start with. A lot more expensive. But it seems to me that the cost don't matter, if you're going to have a tower block that's going to fall down in a few years when, if you'd built it in Portland Stone, it'd be forever like.'

It is easy to wonder how much more stone there is on Portland, or whether Ralph and those who follow him will just go on quarrying away until the Gibraltar of Wessex vanishes into the sea.

With the little dog bounding along at his heels, Ralph Stone heads home for tea up a precipitous path along the edge of the quarry. He turns and looks out to sea, where a frigate is practising tight turns in the brilliant blue water. 'I think it's a good place to live. I've never lived anywhere else I suppose. It's not exactly pretty. But I'm quite 'appy 'ere anyway.'

BECAUSE of their isolation, Portlanders are good at making their own entertainment. And they are proud of their home-grown Morris Dancing team, which performs regularly at the Cove Inn on the edge of the Chesil Beach. The great bank of shingle stretches away into the distance. The sea washes ashore and rolls even smoother sides onto the rounded pebbles. The dancers move back and forth – one of them disguised as a rather improbable sheep. And the musicians, dressed in top-hats and cast-offs, try to hang on to the tune in the blustery, evening breeze. Jan Morgan, pretty as a Dutch doll, comes from one of the houses clinging to the steep hillside.

With her sun-tan and straw hat she dances with skill, determination and great energy.

'One of our favourite dances is called the Jubilee Dance. It was first performed for Queen Victoria's Golden Jubilee in 1886. But there's dances being made up all the time and there's dances that go right back. There's even dances being made up today.'

You get a brisk response from Jan and something a little harder than a twinkle in her eye, if you are bold enough to suggest that Morris Dancing is mainly for men. 'Well, a lot of people seem to think it's just men that are allowed to Morris dance. But women have been dancing Morris for well over a hundred years, and the men seem to think they've got an authority on it. But us women know better. I don't know how many mens' sides there are. I'm not interested. But, across the country, there's about a hundred women's sides.'

Sadly, none of the dances which Jan and her side perform, originate in Portland. But there are dances, which used to be done on the Island, and they hope to be learning them before long. In spite of Jan's protests about men, she and her friends are accompanied by an all male band. 'We have got women musicians. But mostly the women like to dance, so we let the men get on with the music. Some of us are Portlanders. Some of us are Kimberlins that were not born on the Island, but live on the Island. But some of us – just a few – are foreigners, who come in off the mainland.'

The dancers whirl and weave. The spectators sink their pints of local beer. The children eat crisps and clap their hands. And, in the midst of it all, the dancer dressed as a sheep leaps about and gets in everyone's way. 'Most Morris sides have an exotic animal. We chose to have a Portland sheep because Portland's very famous for its fine mutton. Also, the Portland sheep was believed never to be cross-bred, although I'm not quite sure about our Edna. So we chose Edna to come out with us. If it comes out with us, it's definitely female.

'We all love doing it. But it's something you've got to practise hard. We rehearse all winter. We've got to practise a lot to know the steppings. But when we go out in the summer we go out to enjoy ourselves, to be sociable and to have a good time, just as long as we're keeping up the standards that we've been practising all through the winter.'

MUCH of Portland consists of abandoned quarries, into which waste from other quarries has been dumped. Over the decades nature has managed to claw her way back into this devastation, and today many of the old workings are rich with birds, butterflies and flowers. These former quarries are a favourite walking place for local naturalist Margaret Lester and her sleek Red Setter, Emma.

'The landscape of Portland has been created by the quarrying. The hills are not natural hills. They're man-made hills from the spoil from the quarries. Then nature has taken over and covered them with grass, so that they appear to be natural. But obviously they're not. Most of the places Emma and I walk through haven't been worked for fifty or sixty years. They've been left alone during that period, so now life is starting up again. There are plenty of blue butterflies and brimstones, whites and orange-tips – and a whole mass of plant-life too. In the season you find areas carpeted with horseshoe vetch. There's always something new to see or to find.'

Coming over a steep bank Margaret and Emma startle a skewbald mare, tethered to a post, and her young foal foraging nearby. Just beyond them there's a patch of bluish, hairy plants called viper's bugloss – a sure sign that this is adder country. 'We get a lot of adders in the quarries, specially on hot days. Trouble is that they do tend to lay across the paths and sunbathe. So you need to watch your step. But it's worth walking with your eyes on the ground anyway, because, being so close to the sea, there are all sorts of special wild things growing, which you might otherwise miss.'

Off they go through the torn landscape, Emma running ahead and finding excitement over each steep rise and behind every jagged rock.

P ORTLAND, like Gibraltar, is buffeted by high winds and strong currents. It can be bleak and windswept, and its people seem almost to speak a different language from those of us on the mainland. There is a clannishness here, such as is often found on islands, as well as a strong feeling of pride in being part of a small but historic community. People who have been brought up here will not think of living anywhere else, because of the high value they put on the friendship of their neighbours. It is a place where loyalty still matters.

THE ISLE OF PURBECK

IN his book *The Ingrained Island*, Paul Hyland describes the Isle of Purbeck – 'Take an expanse of heath like Hardy's Egdon; set it on the margins of the second largest natural harbour in the world; add the scenery of the Isle of Wight and a strip of valley from the Weald of Kent; buttress it against the sea with Portland stone and a skirt of dark clays; pack all that into an area of sixty square miles, and you have a makeshift recipe for Purbeck.'

Of course, the Isle of Purbeck is not really an island at all. But this contradiction does nothing to stem the flood of fair-weather visitors, who flock here in spring and summer. The northern edge of the area is guarded by the river Frome, which Thomas Hardy pictures in *Tess of the D'Urbervilles* – 'The river itself flows not like the streams in Blackmore. These were slow, silent, often turbid, flowing over a bed of mud, into which the incautious wader might sink unawares. The Frome waters were clear as the pure river of life shown to the Evangelist, rapid as the shadows of a cloud, with pebbly shallows that prattled to the sky all day long.'

The Purbeck Hills cross the Isle from east to west. The northern range, which reaches a height of 600 feet, runs from Ballard Point in the east, by Ballard Down, Nine Barrow Down and Brenscombe Hill to a gap overlooked by the ruin of Corfe Castle. From there it continues westwards by Knowle Hill, Creech Barrow, Povington Hill, Whiteway Hill and on to Rings Hill. The whole length of this journey offers magnificent views across the countryside. The southern range of hills starts at Durlston Head in the east. It passes Anvil Point, St. Aldhelm's Head, Swyre Head, Gad Cliff, Winspit Cove, Chapman's Pool, Kimmeridge Bay, Brandy Bay and ends at Worbarrow Bay in the west. It is in this line of hills that Portland marble and stone are quarried.

To enjoy Purbeck to the full you need to go there out of season to avoid the notorious grockles. Then you can see the superb views, stretching to Portland and the Isle of Wight without a trace of a tent, a caravan or a traffic jam. Somehow, the people of Purbeck seem to have escaped contamination from the outside world, in spite of the annual invasion of city-dwellers in search of their souls.

IN *The Hand of Ethelberta*, Thomas Hardy writes of Knollsea, his name for Swanage – 'Knollsea was a seaside village lying snug between two headlands as between a finger and a thumb. Everybody in the parish, who was not a boatman, was a quarrier, unless he was the gentleman who owned half the property and had been a quarryman, or the gentleman who owned the other half and had been to sea . . . The quarrymen, in white fustian, understood practical geology, the laws and accidents of dips, faults and cleavage, far better than the ways of world and mammon.' Today, Purbeck Stone is still deservedly famous the world over. It is strong, attractive and full of the true worth which architects of most modern buildings seem to despise. Harold Bonfield, big, broad and beefy, lives on the outskirts of Swanage. His family has been quarrying and shaping Portland stone for centuries, and Harold is as solid and as sure as the stone itself.

'They've always called it The Isle of Purbeck 'cos we've got the Wareham river that runs through Wareham and out towards Weymouth. I don't think it's actually an island, but it was always called one. And the Purbeck men were all quarrymen once.'

Harold's family came originally from France, and he has records in the name of Bonneville going back to 1199. He reckons that ancestors of his worked on Corfe Castle and that their abilities have been handed down to him through the generations. 'You need a fair bit of skill to do the job properly. Of course, we've got modern machinery like drills and saws, which help, but you can still make a mess of the stone with them. You've got to have a little bit of knowledge how to do it. There's different veins for different types of stone. For instance, Portland is good stone for the outside of a building. But our stone, from its thinner beds, is a smaller type of stone for inside buildings – fireplaces an' that.'

High on a hill above Swanage and close to a new housing estate, Harold Bonfield still maintains an underground quarry. Old winding gear, chunky chains, dilapidated sheds, solid wooden trolleys and piles of discarded stone surround the deep, dark shaft, which plunges steeply into the hillside. Brambles have fought and twined their way into the workings, but the quarry itself is still open and, carrying candles, it is possible to see the veins of stone and the layers of clay between, and to imagine what it must have been like to mine rocks in the damp and the darkness and the dirt. Heavy work for men, who were built differently from most of today's workers.

'We opened an underground shaft in 1949. We worked down there until 1954. Most of the undergrounds – ten perhaps – we were working between the two wars. But after the last war a lot of the chaps didn't go back to underground. They preferred to work on the surface. There's none actually dug from underground now. All of it comes from open cast quarries.'

Back at the yard, close beside Harold's home, men in goggles chip away at the stone with hammers and chisels. Outside, a huge guillotine thunders and groans as the chains pull the blade skywards before gravity allows it to crash down and split another slab of handsome stone. An old man, his lined face powdered with dust from the stone he is shaping with infinite patience, has the style of a Bonfield about him. 'My father's still alive. He's in his seventies. When I left school I did actually work

Harold Bonfield from Swanage, whose family has been quarrying and shaping Portland Stone for centuries.

with me father underground, and I 'ope to pass all the skills and all the little quiffs about how it goes underground on to my son. And that's how it's been for generations. This place is special to us. There's a tradition in the stone trade and it seems that fathers and their sons carry it on. I don't think any of us would want to be doing it anywhere else.'

THE Purbeck scenery, dominated by Corfe Castle, is spectacular. And its people are constantly reminded of their links with the past by the history that surrounds them. But this has failed to make them too solemn or self-important. If you are lucky you can see this truth demonstrated to perfection beside the river Frome on the fine, old quay at Wareham by the local dance group, the Dorset Buttons, and their dark and elegant leader, Sue Incledon.

'The Dorset Buttons' principle is that we do it because we enjoy it. We're all girls. If the men want to dance, that's fine. And if they don't want to dance with us, that's up to them.'

This segregation of the sexes in dancing comes up again and again in the countryside. The reasons are hard to discover and the feelings about it are strong. But it takes nothing away from the splendour of the setting with the church and the old buildings surrounding the quay, the broad river with its boats and swans to the south and the attractive dancers in their colourful costumes moving backwards and forwards in perfect time to the sound of accordian, violin and pipes. It is a delightful link with the past, which even the passing traffic can do little to spoil. 'The tradition of girls doing the dancing here goes back at least a hundred and fifty years. Some of our dances are from Dorset – simply because we've made them up. Morris dancing itself comes from the North-West and the Cotswolds. The Dorset dances are more like country dancing.'

The paving stones ring with the sound of the girls feet in their heavy shoes and thick stockings, and the pale sunshine throws fantastic shadows as they bend and weave. The spectators huddle in their overcoats and envy the dancers the heat generated by their efforts. And the gulls look on disdainfully from their private perches on the top of the church tower.

STUDLAND Heath takes up nearly five hundred acres on the eastern edge of the Isle of Purbeck and fringing Poole Harbour. It is wonderfully wild country – a haven for seabirds, butterflies, snakes and flowers. It is also home for the much-admired Dartford Warbler. The whole area is treasured by the Senior Warden, Rees Cox, who finds that it compensates him in part for his beloved, native Wales.

'I must admit that sometimes we seem to be glorified gardeners – playing God or interfering with nature or whatever you like. But the heathlands in this part of the world were increased by man many years ago – cutting down the birch woodlands that were here, and making bigger clearings to graze their animals. And, if we now sat back and did nothing to it, it could change back to pine or birch woodland.'

Rees drives across the heath in a Land Rover with a big water tank in the back and an ever-ready hosepipe. Fire is a constant hazard and, in the minutes before the fire engines arrived, he might be able to contain a gorse fire for a few vital moments. But, if time allows, he prefers to walk across his patch, binoculars at the ready and keen eyes scanning the scene for any one of a thousand possible sights. 'Heathlands have a number of plants and animals and insects, which are found nowhere else. The soils are very poor, so not many plants can survive in it. And there are only certain things, like some of the heathers, gorse and a number of the plants that catch insects to feed on, which are restricted to heathland soils. And, of course, associated with them, are the insects and animals, which are found only where those plants are growing.'

There is a story that someone on the Isle of Purbeck once put up a polite notice by the road side which read 'Please do not feed the adders'. Its purpose was to keep the trippers away – and in this it probably succeeded. Studland Heath is alive with adders, though you need sharp eyes, patience and local knowledge to find them. Predictably, Rees Cox's attitude to adders is rather different from the fear and revulsion with which they are viewed by most people. 'They're beautiful really. They vary quite a bit in colour. They can be black and white, rusty browns, yellows, greenish greys, but always with the zig-zag band down the back.'

Without difficulty and with great gentleness he catches an adder. He treats it calmly and with respect. 'You shouldn't do this unless you know what you're about, because they give you a nasty bite. It very rarely kills people, but it can be bad and people have died from it. If I was bitten now I should whistle off to Poole Harbour pretty quickly. But in fact, they're very shy creatures though their diet of baby mice, voles, shrews or baby birds might not make you think so. What is quite wrong is to think that you have got to kill them.'

Down by the waterside there is a well-camouflaged hide, from where you can watch in peace as scores of slim waterbirds feed on the edge of the mud. Behind are the sounds of robins and Dartford Warblers. In front are the haunting cries of the gulls and the waders. 'Poole Harbour is supposed to be the second largest natural harbour in the world. I think Sydney Harbour is the biggest. In the winter we get lots of different birds – black-tailed godwit, mergansers, grey plovers, red-shanks and dunlin. Quite a range really. And keeping an eye on all of them is one of the many good parts of the job.'

THERE are not just cats at the Margaret Green Animal Sanctuary at Church Knowle – though there are 130 of them there. They keep company with a Noah's Ark of creatures of every shape and size. Local girl, Sylvia Dobb, is one of the people who helps look after them all. Slim, blonde and from Weymouth she has to be an expert in everything from seagulls to pit ponies.

'The good thing about the Isle of Purbeck is that it hasn't yet been spoilt by man's improvements, which invariably turn out to be disasters for the wildlife. Also, the local people here have a great regard for the area, and a natural love for and interest in the plants and the creatures. So I think that, as long as the people care, there's always a chance for animals to survive.'

Although looking after the animals is her job, it means far more than that to Sylvia and she is as dedicated to her charges as any Mother Therésa. 'I usually start about 7.30 in the morning and finish between 5.0 and 5.30 in the evening. But I generally have evening duties as well. Because anybody can bring their animals to us at any time of the day or night. Most of them are strays or unwanted. Sometimes it's old people moving into homes or things like that.'

At the bottom end of the sanctuary is a field for donkeys and ponies. Here are quite a number of pit-ponies from the bad old days when they spent their lives underground. The oldest one is from Wales, is called Jolly and is 44 years old.

PURBECK is sheep country. There is probably as much knowledge about wool, mutton, lamb and grassland contained in these stone hills as anywhere else in the country. Billy Kinghorn came to Purbeck from the Isle of Arran in Scotland over twenty years ago. A friend there told him to leave unless he wanted to end up as a shepherd, a fisherman or an alcoholic. So Billy came south and 'became all three'. Today he travels the world shearing sheep as far afield as Rome and the U.S.A. and demonstrating his skills. But his heart and his farm are in the Isle of Purbeck. On a misty Spring morning his lean, hard figure strides down off the hills behind a huge flock of sheep, whose steaming backs add to the fog and make magic of the mass movement.

'I think it's probably the most beautiful place I've ever seen. It's so different from Scotland. It's quieter. It's gentler. It's not so harsh. The weather's better. And I'm very happy in Dorset. I travel everywhere. But my home's in Dorset – in the Purbecks. And I just adore it. It's a wee bit harder down here for us. The lambing percentages we have to get are much higher. Where I come from in Scotland we had 100% lambing on the hills and that was considered good. Down here we've got to have 200 or 210%. That's what we've got to try for. So it makes the job more difficult. We bring them into big sheds here whereas in Scotland – in my day – we didn't have anything like that at all.'

Four or five hundred sheep trot down the old street between the thatched houses just to the north of Lulworth Cove. The collies rush busily up and down keeping order and discipline. The village seems more at ease with the sheep than with the summer tourists – even if they do bring in more cash. 'We've got a bunch of hoggets – that's yearling sheep – and we're going to be dagging them or cleaning them up and clipping them round the tail. We've also got a new scanning machine. We can tell how many lambs each is going to have – or if it's going to have any at all. If we find some that are not going to have lambs we don't need to put them in the sheds, which means more room for the ones which are going to have lambs. This is something very new. We've done about twelve thousand sheep in the last month and it's going to take off in a big way in the future.'

With all those sheep, one problem that Billy Kinghorn does not suffer from is getting to sleep at nights!

LIKE all isolated areas, Purbeck breeds its eccentrics. In the vanguard must be the Muddlecombe Men – a group of local enthusiasts, who perform in pubs and carnivals around the district, and even on a chilly evening outside the Square and Compass Inn at Worth Matravers. Their leader is Hughie Elms from Wareham. He introduces one of their favourite numbers.

'When ten men plucked ten thousand pheasants in fourteen hours they broke a

Though Billy Kinghorn travels the world demonstrating his skill as a sheep shearer, his heart lies on the Isle of Purbeck where he has over 400 sheep on his farm.

record. And that record's never been broken yet, me boys. The Squire was so pleased with 'em he gave 'em a brand new silver piece each, and they went back to the village inn and they had a drink and this dance started. So here they are, Ladies and Gentlemen, the Muddlecombe Men with their Pheasant Pluckers Dance.'

The feathers fly, the beer flows and a good time is had by all. In spite of the frivolity, Hughie is quite serious about Purbeck. 'This place is a way of life for us. It's a peculiar thing and you can't really explain it. It's got strong roots and you're stuck with it. You're there with it. And we're lucky that we live somewhere that has such a strong hold.'

ANY portrait of the Isle of Purbeck has to end with the words of the unchallenged descriptive master of Dorset, Thomas Hardy.

'A valley of heavy greens and browns, which, at its furthest side, rose like knuckles gloved in dark olive, and little plantations between them formed a still deeper and sadder monochrome. A zinc sky met a leaden sea on this hand, the low wind groaned and whined, and not a bird sang.'

THE VALLEY OF THE BRIDE

IN Southern Dorset – just to the East of Bridport – there is an ancient and secret valley, through which the little river Bride tumbles and eddies to the sea at Burton Bradstock. In Celtic 'bridda' means 'gushing' or 'boiling' and, as the stream falls more than two hundred feet in its first three miles, this is a likely explanation for the name. In a document dated 1288 the river is referred to as 'aqua de Brydie' and, even earlier, in 987 A.D. the villages of Longbredy and Littlebredy were called Bridian. The Domesday Book names Longbredy as Langebride, but the word Bredy does not appear in writing until the 15th century. If you visit the area today you will find that local people, with their roots deep in the valley, use the ancient pronunciation 'Briddy' rather than the more recent 'Bredy'. By what means do people living today still retain the sounds of a thousand years ago? But they manage to do it and, if you ask for Longbredy, many will look puzzled until the light dawns and they say, 'Oh, you mean Longbriddy'.

The source of the Bride is at Littlebredy and comes from springs in a lake, which stands before Bridehead House, reputed to be the inspiration for Evelyn Waugh's *Brideshead Revisited*. It is, at any rate, a stately house reflected in the black water of the lake and surrounded by magnificent trees and parkland. The village can have changed little over the centuries and is full of grey stone and thatch. The Bride pours down an Alpine waterfall from the lake and wanders past the cottage gardens on its way to the sea. Unusually, the river has no mouth. It ends in a lagoon and then seeps through the shingle into the sea at Freshwater. This is the western end of the Chesil Beach. The pebbles on the giant bank of shingle are the smallest down here, and become steadily larger as the Chesil reaches out towards Portland.

In *The Spinners*, Eden Philpotts has this charming description of the Bride and the village of Burton Bradstock.

'Bride river winds in the midst, and her bright waters throw a loop round the eastern frontier of the hamlet, pass under the highway, bring life to the cottage gardens and turn more wheels than one. Bloom of apple and pear are mirrored on her face, and fruit falls into her lap in autumn time. Then westward she flows through the water meadows, and so slips uneventfully away to sea, where the cliffs break and there stretches a little strand. To the last she is crowned with flowers, and the meadowsweets and violets that decked her cradle give place to sea poppies, sea

The source of the Bride is at Littlebredy and comes from springs in a lake at Bridehead House, reputed to be the inspiration for Evelyn Waugh's *Brideshead Revisited*.

hollies and stones encrusted with lichens of red gold, where Bride flows to one great pool, sinks into the sand and glides unseen to her lover.'

THIS is strong and old-fashioned dairy country. Cows have fed on the gentle hills for centuries. And one of the rarest and finest British cheeses – Dorset Blue Vinney – comes from these parts. Under the watchful eye of Mike Harp at Ashley Chase Dairy, tons of less exotic but just as delicious cheese are made today. Huge, stainless steel paddles stir a sea of milk in a bath, which would comfortably house two rugger teams. Men in white overalls and caps plunge their arms into the liquid

The common frog (*Rana Temporaria*) photographed basking in the sun by his Dorset pond. They are found throughout Britain, usually near water and damp undergrowth.

The small pearl-bordered fritillary butterfly can be seen in woodland clearings from June–September, though they will settle on grassy paths in overcast weather. This one was photographed near Littlebredy in Dorset.

and mix and stir. Later they carve the solidifying material with giant knives and slap and pummel the rubbery chunks. Water and steam gush and roar and the action and industry are non-stop.

'I start at four in the morning and the rest start at five. The reason is that we have to pasteurize the milk first. So that has to be started early, and then there's enough for everyone else to do during their eight-hour working day. At the moment we're producing 4,300 gallons of our own milk each day. We make that into cheese over a six day period, which means that we're making just over two tons a day. It's a cheddar cheese and a very good one too I might add.'

On a modest assembly line wooden boxes queue up to be pressed full of fresh cheese. In a nearby store pyramids of boxes stand maturing while, elsewhere, the

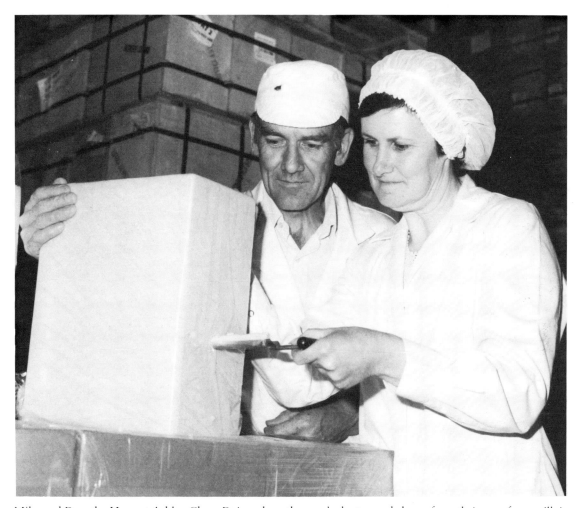

Mike and Dorothy Harp at Ashley Chase Dairy where they make butter and cheese from their own farm milk in the traditional manner.

finished product, which was turned into cheese over a year ago, is wrapped and packed ready to start its journey to the shops and to hungry mouths all over the country. 'Making good cheese is not so much a craft. It's more of a skill if you like. It has a taste and a feel more than anything. I reckon I can make good cheese here, but if I went into the next county or even the next farm to make cheese perhaps I wouldn't get on quite so well. It varies from county to county and farm to farm.'

While the rest of the team is busy with the cheese, Mike Harp's wife, Dorothy, is in charge of butter production. A busily revolving churn shudders to a halt and she reaches in to bring out a giant mound of dark yellow butter. She weighs the lumps with care as she pulls them off, and then pats them into delicate and uniform curled shapes. Mike is proud of her ability.

'She starts at 7.30. By that time the butter will be churned. There are only three types of wood you can use for butter pats – beech, box or holly. They're all ideal for butter, because they don't splinter and leave little bits of wood all over the place. If you use metal, then in the winter the pats get too cold and the butter will harden and stick, and in the summer they conduct too much heat and the butter will melt. So it's got to be wood. And a light one too. You couldn't have an old piece of elm because, after a while, the weight of it would break your wrists.'

Across the valley the sun shines on the old hills. The greystone farm houses stand as they have for hundreds of years, and the cows graze and chew the cud preparing their milk for the next day's run on the cheese assembly line. Spare them and the workers at Ashley Chase Dairy a thought next time you buy a vacuum-packed chunk of cheddar at the local supermarket.

SHEEP mix cheerfully with cattle in the Bride Valley, and sheep dogs and shepherds abound. On the low hills with their steep sides a good, woolly coat is an essential part of survival in the fierce winter weather that roars in from the west. John Randall from Litton Cheney is a shepherd, who has won many prizes at the Royal Show and Smithfield, but his heart is in the valley with his sheep and his dogs.

'I've been farming sheep in this area for forty years, I suppose. I've played about with heavy horses and cows, but it's been sheep for most of the time. It's a Garden of Eden – the Bride Valley. Best area going in England they used to reckon. And it still is, I think.'

John is tall, well-built and handsome, with a wise, country face and honest eyes. He wears leather gaiters and boots, an old, tweed jacket and a battered, felt hat. 'As a young man virtually all the sheep in this area were either Dorset Downs or Dorset Horns. They were running on these steep slopes during the day and folded at nights on the chalkland on the tops. It was the only way you could grow corn on this chalk arable – to feed the steep banks that you couldn't plough and bring the manure back onto the flat ground at night.'

John's two sheepdogs race up the hill to round up the flock. But the sheep are well-trained and seem to know precisely what is expected of them. In the distance a fine, young stag breaks cover from a rough thicket in a dip of the downs and vanishes over the skyline without looking back. John barks orders at the dogs, which lie close to the ground trembling with suppressed energy. The sheep quietly pack into the fold.

'Nowadays it's all and sundry as far as the breeds are concerned. The Downs and Horns have all gone. Now it's mostly Mules around here and Scotch half-breds and all the other crosses. A fat lamb job. It's a great tragedy really, innit? Great tragedy. I often say now to the young people that there aren't any more real shepherds today. They buy their female replacements. They buy the rams. They put 'em together and they sell fat lambs. And, at the end of the day, they start all over again. Whereas in our days, it was continuity that counted. You bred your ewe lambs. You kept your female replacements back and you know, at the end of ten years, you had something to look at. You'd bred that flock of sheep.'

While John examines and treats the feet of a lame ewe with a ferocious mixture of burnt bluestone, antimony, spirit of lead and lard, he reflects on the sources of some of the old country legends, for which this part of Dorset is famous. 'You know, in most of the old places which have their old stories and their old traditions, the people used to fill themselves up with local cider years ago, so it wasn't so surprising what they used to see at night when they were coming back from the pub. This mixture I'm putting on their feet is nearly as strong as the cider too. It's as old as the 'ills that is. I learnt that one over forty years ago off an old shepherd. It still works too. At least, it cures foot rot.'

In a small shed, not far from his home at Litton Cheney, is a pen of pedigree lambs. John's next job is to trim and tidy them for showing. Each lamb is taken out of the pen in turn and tied securely with its chin held up on a metal plate. They stand there as smart and as straight as guardsmen. 'I always reckon that the pedigree job consists of four arts. First of all you have to learn the way to breed 'em. Then you have to learn the way to feed 'em. Then you have to know how to turn 'em out. And last you have to put 'em in that ring and show them to advantage. You've got to combine the four. You can't take each one in isolation. And, of course, presentation's half the art of selling anything, innit? But doing this used to make the job really worthwhile in the old days. Shepherding a folded flock was a terrific lot of hard work. But you used to look forward to the summer shows. You went away for weeks at a time in those days – five or six shows in the summer. Great lot of chaps they were. I was very lucky. I was about when what I would call the last generation of the great shepherds was around. That's where I learned my trade too. And the only place you'll find them now is up in the church yard unfortunately. It's a pity. A great pity.' And, with a sigh, John Randall turns back to his lambs, and applies nearly half a century of skill and experience to turning them into show-pieces.

THE local stone in the Valley of the Bride has gone into the building of all the old houses. Farmers were only too glad to have the rocks taken away from their fields, where they would break ploughshares and lame horses. As a result the old homes and churches blend into the serene beauty of the valley. Whatever the problems facing them, modern architects have failed to take note of this simple fact, and have already built too many of their favourite monstrosities in this lovely area. The stone is also used to build the drystone walls along the borders of the fields, and the difficult job of keeping these walls in good repair is in the skilled hands of men like Roger Day from Burton Bradstock. It is a cold and lonely job and one which demands a good deal of patience.

'The first thing is to get a good base to the wall. You must have a good base, otherwise nothing will stand up.'

Roger chips at the heavy base stones until they fit snugly against one another in two lines on either side of the hole in the broken wall. Then he begins to fill the space in the middle with smaller stones, pushing them tightly together. 'All the infill must be ground in nice and tight. It has to be built up strongly, so that it adds strength to the wall. Mending a wall, where a section has fallen down, is a bit more difficult than making a new wall, because you've got to blend each end to match what is already there on either side of the gap. It's surprising, but sometimes it's better with a little bit of twist in it than trying to keep it in a straight line.'

Miles of grey, stone walls stretch in all directions. Dairy cows, beef cattle and sheep graze in the fields. Sometimes the walls collapse because of the weight of tractors, lorries and farm machinery pushing down the road close beside them. The walls were built before the arrival of such heavy vehicles in the countryside. But sometimes it is the animals themselves, which are responsible. 'Traditionally it's a sheep area round here. The trouble today is that you get all these big steers come along, and they rub on the top of the walls. Now the real dry wall's got no mortar in it at all. All you need to build it is your hands, a shovel, pick and a hammer. You shouldn't need anything else at all. But today we have to use some mortar because of the cattle rubbing on the top. We never had that problem with sheep because they can't reach.'

Roger is well aware of the links which his work gives him with the distant past. 'Some of these walls date back to the Domesday Book. They were parish boundary walls then. There's also parts of Roman walls about in different places. Yes, they're quite old. And, when you get one of those fall over, I think sometimes it's been there long enough.'

As the light begins to fade, the lone figure bends back to his work, the metallic click of stone against stone echoes over the silent valley and, at the foot of the hill, the river Bride moves softly on towards the sea.

RABBITS can sometimes be found sheltering in the stone walls of the valley. But, on a raw November day, they are more likely to be deep in their burrows in the steep banks above Manor Farm at Longbredy. There is nothing quite like free food, and so farm worker Charlie Pitcher takes time off when he can to go ferreting. He is a figure straight out of a Thomas Hardy Novel. He has a strong Dorset accent, a bent back and hands and a face, which have endured decades of hard, outdoor work. The three, white ferrets with their beady, pink eyes are kept in a home-made shed behind Charlie's house in the village. There is an unkempt orchard with windfalls still rotting on the frozen ground. And Charlie is accompanied by his fresh-faced grandson and a fat Jack Russell terrier, which is so excited that it seems tempted to mistake the ferrets for rabbits.

'You know, you've got to handle ferrets when they're young. You must pick 'em up as much as you can, and then they're quiet enough. Occasionally you'll get one that'll bite, but you ain't got to take any notice of 'em. But they'll go for some people. Now one of my sons can't do anything with 'em – for what reason I don't know really. But I can do anything with 'em. You hear about people putting them inside their shirts, or anything like that. I could put them inside of mine. They wouldn't take any notice.'

'Sometimes you get the ferrets lost up 'ere and leave 'em 'ere, you know. Then you put the ferret's box with a little drop of milk in a saucer and come back up in two or three days time, and you'll find 'em curled up in the box. Sometimes you lose 'em altogether, but not very often. I had one lost up 'ere for a week, you know, and then, if you're down in the village, you can see 'em walking about. That's the best with having the white ones. You can see 'em up there. Though the black-and-white ones are quicker – a lot quicker – than the white ones.'

Like so many old-timers Charlie Pitcher regrets the old days. The work may have been harder, longer and colder, but life was more friendly.

'I've been on this farm 'ere for such a long time. When I started work there was six or seven of us 'ere working. Now there's only the three of us. Used to come out 'ere hoein' with the six of us all in a line. And now you go up there with a tractor on your own. That's all. There isn't so much company now as it used to be by a long ways. Not so much fun either I don't think. You know, we always used to be up to some nonsense. Never been very far away from here at all. No. Been in a train twice – that's all – in my life – and that's only from Dorchester to Maiden Newton. I've hardly been out of the county. I like it 'ere in the village.' And the old voice drifts softly away as he turns back to the boy and the rabbits.

AT Bredy Farm, near Burton Bradstock, there is every kind of activity, and farm carpenter and wheelwright, Ray Tompkins, is at the centre of much of it. Whether he is high up a ladder wielding a heavy hammer and building a fine barn miles from anywhere or in his snug workshop making an elegant chair or table, you can be sure that most areas of farm life bear his mark.

'This is the life. I've never known nothing else, you see. And I don't mind where I work with wood, or whether the weather's cold or hot. I'd rather be outside working. It would be horrible to be in a factory – just not my life at all. I enjoy timber – anything to do with wood I like. And I like the hardwoods – elm being my

The Bride valley in southern Dorset, off the main tourist routes, remains unspoilt by the intrusions of the twentieth century.

favourite wood really. The colouring's good, the grain's nice, it works beautiful and it does look fine when it's finished. I think it was a shame when all the elms had Dutch Elm Disease and they had to be felled. People were sawing them up for firewood. And it's wrong really. I think they should be turned into something useful – objects of value and beauty. That's what they grew there for.'

70

As he works, Ray Tompkins is surrounded by his creations – a fine table, wooden stools and benches, an intricate loom, an undertaker's bier as well as by all the tools of his trade. At the far end of the building, where his workshop is situated, a large man in a tartan cap is in charge of a colossal horizontal saw. This is Norman Legg and he is busily turning tree trunks into stout planks for barn-building. In another farm shed Cyril Standley is wood-turning and creates goblets, lamps, rolling-pins and egg-cups out of local timber. These men have begun to achieve on one farm the kind of industry that once was common across the valley.

'Everybody knew everybody in the little villages, you know, years ago. Unfortunately that's changed now. Each village had a wheelwright and a carpenter. I knew them all. There was blacksmiths and stonemasons and undertakers. Each one of us did our own undertaking. Now there's no undertaker, nor any of the others either. And life has changed really.'

In the orchard beside The Bride men are picking apples and carrying them to a noisy barn, where cider is being made. As the fruit is poured into a funnel at the top of a belt-driven grinding-machine, there is a sharp change of sound and a mass of shredded apple pours down into the wooden trough below. The apple sludge is then shovelled into the ancient press, which stands against the back wall. Sacking is wrapped round the pulverised fruit and pressure exerted with the help of a five-foot spanner, which is used to wind the press down. Juice trickles and then pours into a waiting bath.

'Immediately opposite the door of my house in Litton Cheney was a purpose-built cider house. And there's still lots of cider made here in the valley, although it's not a true cider area really. But each farmer had a small orchard, and they all used to produce a little drop. So we still make it on the farm here. They tell me it's good. But I don't really drink it.'

IF you have the time and the inclination to turn off a main road in Dorset and to travel down unmarked lanes into the Bride Valley during the cold part of the year, you will find the whole place tucked up and tidy and ready for the winter. And you will still be able to catch a glimpse of the Dorset countryside as it was described by that great countryman, Ralph Wightman.

'There are amazing colours, curious lights and shadows, veils of mist, which leave Golden Cap floating insubstantial as a dream island. In a thousand journeys you will never see this land twice the same. It is Merlin's magic earth, a precious stone, the walls of England and the fields of home.'

CRANBORNE CHASE

CRANBORNE Chase stretches across 150,000 acres of Dorset, Hampshire and Wiltshire and is framed on its four corners by Shaftesbury, Salisbury, Ringwood and Wimborne. It was a hunting forest from the Norman Conquest up until the reign of the Stuarts, and was conveniently situated – for those on the stag-hunting circuit – between the New Forest, Gillingham Forest and the Forest of Blackmoor. But, without the consent of the Lord of the Chase, no one was allowed to interfere with the trees and bushes in the area because they provided food for the deer. The ban on clearing the woodland gave big problems to local farmers, who wanted to create fields. Travellers were also obliged to pay a toll for crossing Cranborne Chase during the breeding season, since their movement could disturb the hinds and fawns.

Thomas Hardy described Cranborne Chase in *Tess of the D'Urbervilles*. 'A truly venerable tract of forest land, one of the few remaining woodlands in England of undoubted primaeval date, wherein druidical mistletoe was still found on aged oaks, and where enormous yew-trees, not planted by the hand of man, grew as they had grown when they were pollarded for bows.' Today, much of the woodland has disappeared. But there remains an outstandingly beautiful stretch of rolling, English countryside interwoven by tiny lanes with wild flowers growing on either side.

Two-thirds of all the types of British butterflies can be found in the area. White Admirals, which elsewhere would turn a head, seem almost commonplace, and the hedgerows and banks are alive with creatures of every shape and description.

Because of its history as a Forest of the Chase, there are no large towns. But the tiny villages, scattered across the downland, are as charming as you can find anywhere else in the country. Everywhere there are comfy thatched cottages, and the mediaeval atmosphere has remained surprisingly uncontaminated by modern life.

THE people of Cranborne Chase seem confident and secure in the history and tradition which surround them. There is no industry here, and the calm is a dramatic contrast to the strident world on all sides. Mark Harris from Farnham has spent his 72 years in the Chase, much of it as a hurdle-maker. Today, he still manages to make his skilled trade look relatively simple. But, as the years pass and youthful strength wanes, he now chooses thinner sticks, with which to weave his intricate patterns.

'I've worked in the woods all me life. Fifty-seven years now. I learnt hurdle-makin' off me uncle. And I started work with him and I've worked in these woods over the years now – except for a while during the War when I was in the Coldstream Guards.'

Mark seems too frail to have been a guardsman. He fits so neatly into the woods that it is hard to believe that he has ever left them. With the sun shining through the leaves and bracken making dappled patterns on the forest floor, Mark remembers the annual wood sale, which used to be held at a hotel in nearby Farnham.

'It happened every November and it was called the Woodman's Derby Day. The hotel was open from 10 o'clock in the morning until 10 o'clock at night. A week or two before the sales the estate woodmen used to measure out the woods. They'd calculate each lot and sell it by the perch. And then they had it printed on catalogues. Of course, you'd know exactly what you was buying, even though you was at the hotel, because you 'ad a chance to look all round these woods, which 'ad different names and you'd pick out what you fancy you wanted and, of course, they'd sell it to the highest bidder.'

It's quiet in the woods. There are no sounds of traffic or aeroplanes; just the songs of birds and the regular thud of Mark's hand-axe as he works. 'There was more than twenty hurdle-makers about 'ere then on the Estate, and they'd all buy the wood and manufacture it themselves, you see. It was mostly sheep-hurdles in them days and then the sheep died out and the garden-fence hurdles came in. A lot of the hurdle-makers died and no young ones took it on, but you couldn't much blame 'em because it's a monotonous job up in the wood all day. No one to speak to sometimes.'

The wood sales were one of the great social events of the year for Mark and his fellow-workers. 'There were as many as sixty or seventy people there. Of course, then it dwindled down to about four or five hurdle-makers left 'ere, and then it wasn't worth having a sale any more. I think they gave up about twelve years ago. So now we do it privately. The only thing that hasn't changed is the hazel wood itself. It needs to be anything from 10, 15 up to 20 years old. But I don't want anything too big now at my age. Of course, we used to cut all the woods here by hand – all the big stuff too. We had to in them days. But now the chain-saw has come in, which is a good thing I suppose, and we cut the big stuff with them now.'

There is sadness and regret in the way Mark Harris talks. Life may be easier for him now, but he gives the impression that there is less pleasure in it than in the past. Whatever the truth of that, the standard of his work remains as high as ever and, to many of those who earn their living in the towns and cities, he would seem to have an idyllic job in a perfect setting.

THE centre of village life in the 1980s is more likely to be the pub than the church. The local beer in Cranborne Chase is something special, and Tom Bath, the publican of the Horseshoe Inn at Ebbesbourne Wake, is a little bit out of the ordinary as well. His bar is a magnet for the people of the area and his vegetable garden and his ducks are a permanent reminder of his early life as a farm worker in the Chase. Tom is a big man with a shiny, bald head. He grunts and groans as he rolls the heavy barrels of beer across the yard from his cellar to the pub, and he pauses from time to time to wipe the sweat from his face.

'This little village of ours, we've been lucky because there's not been any sort of development, really. So the village is more or less what it was. There's less people here than when I was a youngster. But the actual village itself is not really changed at all. When I went to school here there was anything from sixty to eighty children – that was just from Ebbesbourne and a few from the next village, Alvediston. Now, with the addition of Berwick St. John, there's less than twenty. Yeah, and when I was a youngster I can remember when we used to play football we often used to have fourteen on each side. Now we've got a little football team in the village today, and our lads have got to import players to make up eleven.'

Tom is proud of the strength and the taste of the beer he sells. He takes infinite trouble to ensure that everything is just right. And, in the old-fashioned bars, he makes a stately progress from customer to customer to ensure that everyone is conent. 'It's a good drop of beer – and it's good for you too. Builds up your muscles. The locals give me a lot of stick about having a big stomach. But then that's the fault of the customers, because they buy me the beer and so I've got to drink it. What else can I do with it apart from tipping it down the drain? And I'm not going to do that – it's too good. So I drink it and put on a big waist.'

At the bottom of the long, steep garden behind the pub, Tom feeds his ducks and collects the eggs. On the way back up the hill he stops to admire the rows of fine vegetables – onions, carrots, beetroot, beans and cabbages – which help add class to his popular pub lunches. 'Before I started this job I was lucky and became a farm worker. I worked with cattle most of the time. That was seven days a week, of course. So when I became a publican it didn't really worry me, because I was used to working Saturdays and Sundays and that sort of thing. So I was lucky in that respect. If I had to go back, I'd prefer to go back to working on the farms how it was years ago. Mind you, I think the lads on the farms today are just as skilled. But they're skilled in different ways. We were skilled in making a haystack, or thatching, hoeing or ploughing with horses. It was more manual, more physical work on the farm – like threshing and all that sort of thing. Whereas now it's all mechanical – tractors and so on. In my day, if you worked three or four miles from the village you had to cycle or walk. And that was in my life-time.'

If you ask Tom Bath whether he has any complaints about his way of life, he thinks long and hard before he answers. 'If there was one little grumble I'd say that sometimes at half-past six in the evening when you're sat there, you look at the clock and you think, "Oh I must get up and open the pub". And then sometimes you think to yourself, "I just wish I could stay for another ten minutes or quarter of an hour". But that's gone in no time. And the only other thing is that there are a few customers who would like me to stay open after hours. But I have to say to them that what they forget is that tomorrow night they can sit watching television with their feet up. But I've still got to be behind the bar.' And Tom trudges off to join in a darts match and to keep the glasses full.

THE age of elegance is alive and well in Cranborne Chase, and local people regularly keep the old traditions going, as they dance the ancient Dorset ritual dances in the lovely local gardens. The backdrop is an old, white thatched house, built in an L. Underfoot is fine, summer grass. And behind the house is a calm lake, full of lilies and fish and ducks and reflections of the evening sky and the surrounding trees. Music is provided by an enthusiastic fiddler. The dance is called Dorset Triumph, and farmer, Michael Coward, is proud to be involved. 'We dance to enjoy ourselves. These dances are three or four hundred years old, and the people always danced when they were happy. When the spring came along and at Harvest Festival times; those were the occasions people danced. Food was scarce in those days, so they danced when the crops were being sown and especially when they were harvested.'

If it was not for the distant sound of a motor car and the occasional flash of denim among the dancers, it would be possible to imagine that you had gone back two, three or even four hundred years. Certainly, some of those dancing can trace their ancestry back that far in the Chase. And, although the scenery has changed and there is far less woodland than of old, the rolling hills and the little cottages still make it possible to imagine the days when dancing in the garden was the peak of local entertainment.

'There's a little story about this dance – Dorset Triumph. The first man makes advances to the second lady, and then the second corners do the same. The first man runs off down the middle with the second lady, and her partner chases her. They come back in triumph and then they all walk down together, which reconciles the situation. It's a courting dance. Of course, dancing is often to do with courting and this particular one is taken out of Thomas Hardy's manuscripts. Peter Swann, our fiddler, discovered it about twenty years ago and we've been dancing it regularly ever since. It's associated with social gatherings and weddings. It's a very graceful dance. There's a note for every step and the rhythm is wonderful. This is what is so delightful about these dances. You're playing with music. Your feet are the musical instruments and they interpret the music.'

On they dance into the sunset and who would dare suggest that their pleasure is less than the plastic joys of so many contemporary entertainments?

MUCH of Cranborne Chase is owned and farmed by Michael Pitt-Rivers, whose particular pride are his magnificent Arab horses. The finest stallion, head and tail held high and nostrils flaring, is so fine and fierce and fit that he seems to be almost a different breed of animal. The quality of the horses is such that Princes of

Arabia are among those from around the world who come shopping for steeds at the Tollard Park Stud at Tollard Royal. Julie Heald from darkest Manchester is one of the girls who look after these aristocratic creatures. Short and dark and dedicated, she is clearly one of those city people who should have been born in the country.

'It's totally different to what I've been used to. I was a typical townie and this is the first place where I've been right in the middle of nowhere. Town life is completely different from country life – everybody is so spread out. We all meet down at the local pub every Friday night, and yet most of the day you won't see hardly anybody. You're just left to your horses, and everybody else gets on and does their bit on the farm or whatever.'

Julie's northern accent sounds pleasantly out of place in the smooth southern surroundings. Her eyes shine as she speaks of her work in the midst of such special scenery. 'A lot of people get absolutely floored by horsey work. But we're left to do our horses and we enjoy doing them. Naturally, there's the hard side of it. The showing season can be pretty difficult and very long hours. And the foaling is heavy. But it's all so varied that you can't get bored with it.'

When the foals are being born Julie and her friends at the Stud do not get much sleep. 'We're getting thirteen or fourteen foals a year now. We all get up. One of us will have been sitting up with the mares at night. But, as soon as she starts, everybody gets rung round and we all come in and watch it every time. So she has quite an audience. And we have a few cameras out, but not too much to disturb the mare. But it's good, because every foal is different, and the first impressions are the ones that stick in your mind for later on in their lives. You always find yourself thinking back to what they looked like when they were tiny.'

Julie is responsible for showing *Elijah*, the prized stallion and the pride of the Stud. Sometimes he is flown overseas to show himself off. He towers over the girl, but she appears to have no fear at all as she encourages him to hold his head high. 'He's a grand horse to handle. He had his problems of course. But now he's turning out to be just what we wanted. And we've had quite a bit of success with him already. At his first few shows he was fidgety. He didn't want to stand still. He was too busy looking around him. But now he's getting to be a perfect showman – a real show-off in fact. Every time someone flashes a camera he's got to be looking that way. So slowly he's getting educated and his character is coming out.'

And with a clanking of buckets and a few firm words to her high-born charges, Julie vanishes into the stables to continue her hard day's work.

T HE wood of Cranborne Chase has been used by the local people over the centuries to build their houses and their furniture, as well as by archers and pikemen for their weapons. The area has produced many fine craftsmen, and this tradition is carried on today by Cecil Colyer from the workshop behind his home at Shillingstone. A former schoolmaster, his concentration is intense as he bends over his workbench and turns fine wood, as well as sterling silver, into works of art.

The beautiful and peaceful village of Ashmore stands on the hill which is the boundary of Dorset. From here there are breathtaking views of Cranborne Chase.

'When I was younger, I didn't find such fascination in woodwork. But, during the war, I found that I wanted to make things with my hands. So I began to learn how to use wood and how to work a lathe. I do a lot now with new wood, because I like the colour. And then people see what I've made and say, "Will you make me one like that?" But I suppose that, if I'd made them out of mahogany, they would probably have said that they liked that too.'

The wood shavings churn out in a miniature avalanche as Cecil starts work on another delicate wooden bowl. The colours and the grain of the wood glow and contrast as the shape begins to form. 'The easy mistake to make when you're turning wood is to go through the bottom of the bowl. If you do make a hole, the only thing you can do is to throw the bowl away or to pretend that it was designed like that to let the dust fall through! I use local wood. I can get it cheaply. Sometimes people living round about give it to me. And years ago I bought a whole batch, and I've got that seasoning out in the garden.'

The workshop is an organised chaos of tools, drawings, half-finished work, sawdust and shavings and all the paraphernalia of creative work. 'I am very interested in the way things are made and that's why I tend to collect tools – as you see if you look round the workshop. And I also make tools of my own as well — special equipment for the lathe and so on.'

Cecil makes shining and delicate silver goblets as well as bowls and furniture. Sometimes he combines the two crafts and produces delightful wooden vessels with silver linings and decorations.

'If you've been working at a set of chairs and you've been on the planing machine all day long and it's dusty, it's pleasant to sit down and tap away at a bit of silver for a change. On the other hand, if you've been polishing a set of goblets, it's good to get back to carpentry for a while. You've got to be very careful and alert with the high-speed polisher, because, if you catch it, the goblet will leap across the floor and it may not be the same shape when you pick it up.'

He finishes the beaker and, with great precision and care, bends forward to punch his own sponsor's mark onto the silver. It's expensive material and any mistake will be costly. But, with the experience of a lifetime's work behind him and the patience of a true craftsman, mishaps are rare for Cecil Colyer.

CRANBORNE Chase is an example of the English countryside in its perfection. All fears and arguments to the contrary, there is still much that is unspoilt, much that is beautiful and much that is unchanged. But there is a special quality about the Chase — something that is very ancient, very secure and full of the tradition which has made this country strong and successful in the past. There is a sense of timelessness and self-confidence in the villages and in the tiny, country lanes. And there is a feeling of something which even the greed of modern man will find it difficult to destroy — a sense of permanence and strength.'

INDEX